Rodger Ward's GUIDE TO GOOD DRIVING

Rodger Ward's GUIDE TO GOOD DRIVING

BY RODGER WARD
AND BROCK YATES

*Illustrated with photographs
and with drawings by Gordon Bruce*

PUBLISHED IN COOPERATION WITH
THE NATIONAL SAFETY COUNCIL

*Harper & Row, Publishers
New York, Evanston, and London*

RODGER WARD'S GUIDE TO GOOD DRIVING was originally published by Harper & Row in 1963.

First PERENNIAL LIBRARY edition published 1964 by Harper &
Row, Publishers, Incorporated, New York, Evanston, and
London.

Library of Congress catalog card number: 62-8875

CONTENTS

CONTENTS

Rodger Ward's GUIDE TO GOOD DRIVING

1

A FEW
INITIAL CONSIDERATIONS

Some may think it rather strange that a professional race driver is coauthoring a book devoted to the safe and proper operation of a passenger automobile.

Most of us have gained our image of a race driver from what we have read in the newspapers and popular magazines. We picture the competition driver as a man who handles a car with careless desperation, careening about with only the vaguest thread of control over his vehicle.

This is sheer nonsense. Driving a powerful racing car at high speeds takes the most acute kind of control, requiring a judgment and a feel for driving that surpass anything encountered in normal highway motoring. No racing driver ever attained greatness on the basis of sheer nerve or aggressiveness any more than an all-pro fullback has achieved immortality with only brute strength and a willingness to crash against opposing linemen.

It certainly is not the mission of this book to teach the reader how to power slide his car or how to negotiate, at 135 mph, a sweeping bend of the type found at the Indianapolis Motor Speedway. But, by applying some of the techniques used in traveling, turning and stopping at racing speeds to the demands of the highway, we feel the reader can learn some valuable lessons. Today too many motorists on the road do not have the slightest notion of driving technique. They have no idea how a little study of these basic theories of controlling an automobile can add to their pleasure and safety behind the wheel.

Driving should be looked upon as an enjoyable and stimulating challenge to both the mind and body. When done properly, it can be one of the most delightful pastimes of contemporary living. When done carelessly or with fearful restraint it can be a nightmare.

As in any art, driving requires a careful schooling in fundamentals. None of us would expect to play the violin without first learning the musical scale, nor would we hope to paint like Van Gogh without becoming thoroughly familiar with the theories of color. By the same token, becoming a first-class driver must begin with a familiarity with the forces which make a car operate effectively. In music we must learn to control sound, in art color must be controlled, and in driving the factor to be controlled is of course the automobile itself.

By "controlling" an automobile we do not refer to the ability to parallel park or make a right-hand turn at an intersection. Of course these elements of driving are important, but they must be subordinated to such

4

essentials as steering, braking, gear changing and cornering.

Each year about 40,000 of our citizens lose their lives in auto accidents. Naturally this is a shocking and tragic total, but what about the people who survive? There are over 87 million licensed drivers in the United States today and the figure is steadily increasing. Additionally millions more ride in buses and cars annually, making the toll of 40,000 amazingly low (but of course still shameful, because so many accidents could have been avoided).

Contrary to general opinion, the death rate is going *down*. For example, in the late 1930's, less than half the number of drivers of today were on the roads and yet an average of 35,000 people died each year even then! In other words, the number killed annually has remained relatively constant for the past twenty years while the number of active drivers has leap-frogged by the millions.

From this must come one irrefutable conclusion: driving *is* becoming safer. A heavy percentage of the reduction in death toll can be traced to safer vehicles and radically improved highways. Giant strides have been taken in building more reliable automobiles with better lights, brakes and suspensions and in designing smooth, open roads with excellent marking and wide shoulders.

Unfortunately, little has been done to improve our drivers. Aside from the wonderfully worthwhile driver

5

training programs in our schools, very little effort is made to assure that America's motorists are qualified to drive.

Naturally our law-enforcement agencies and safety organizations are striving to correct this situation. More rigid requirements, with periodic retests, are being recommended and will probably be effected in many states. Many complain that a majority of the current tests are based on an ability to recite rules and to perform minimal, low-speed-traffic exercises. Briefly, no check is made of the applicant's ability to *control* his car.

The fundamentals of control, like the table of elements in chemistry, are the essence of driving. Without this knowledge, a driver is headed for trouble no matter how cautiously he drives or how familiar he is with the regulations. But once the basics are learned, the way is clear for safer, more satisfying driving.

We are an unusual nation in that so much of our culture revolves around the automobile. The sales of new cars have an enormous impact on the well-being of our economy. And much has been written in recent years about the automobile as a symbol of status or social position in the United States. The car has, or will have, a great influence on the lives of nearly every one of our 180 million citizens. To many a car means genuine convenience and enjoyment. To others it is the cause of a great financial outlay, with years of stiff monthly payments. And for some the automobile is a symbol of heartbreak and destruction (it has been determined that one member of every basic family group will be injured in a traffic accident—an extremely sobering statistic).

It is ironic how such an influential item as a car can be used so negligently by so many otherwise cautious people. It is probably safe to say that Americans take more risks behind the wheel than at any other time in their lives. A person who would not think of swimming in deep water or walking in the rain without rubbers often will not hesitate to gamble the lives of himself and his passengers by passing on a blind hill.

Many drivers take risks without realizing the potential dangers. The modern car, with its silence and comfort, creates a false sense of security, encouraging some to overextend themselves. In these cases the driver is responsible for an inexcusable ignorance of the capabilities and limitations of his equipment.

A good driver does not take risks and therefore has no need to voluntarily confront real danger. Our nation's highways are not bull rings, where we all must prove ourselves in the face of peril. They more closely resemble a giant chessboard or golf course where an unending chain of mental challenges arise and must be solved. Driving is essentially an activity of the mind and our bodies are important only in that they translate the impulses of our thoughts as we meet and attempt to solve the challenges of the road.

This book reveals no secrets. There are no formulas for making you a better driver in ten simple lessons. Like most things that require genuine skill, no short cuts to success exist. Becoming a good driver takes effort and a sincere desire to learn, and we hope that for some this book will ignite an interest in driving as a demanding and highly satisfying art. Once this ignition point is reached, driving can be viewed in a different light. The drudgery, the fear, the urge to command attention behind the wheel should disappear, to be replaced with a healthy respect for the passenger automobile and the skill involved in controlling it efficiently and safely.

2

SOME SUBTLE BASICS

When a person slips behind the wheel of an automobile, he should, in a certain sense, become a part of the machine.

If the driver is both physically and mentally able to fulfill his end of the partnership, the automobile will in turn give forth its best effort. The key to the entire operation of driving is the driver. An excellent driver can offset a poor automobile but an excellent automobile can seldom offset a poor driver.

Many of us tend to oversimplify the job, interpreting the role of the driver as one involving elementary movements of the ignition switch, throttle, steering wheel, pedals, etc. What is generally ignored is that there is a right and wrong way to make these movements and that the incorrect manipulation of these controls can have a decided effect on your driving.

We have encountered dozens of times, on TV and in Western novels, observations on how someone "sits a horse." An expert can tell a great deal about the proficiency of a rider merely from the way he sits his saddle. By the same token, an expert driver can tell a great deal about a person's ability behind the wheel merely from the way "he sits a car."

If one hunches over the wheel or slumps in the left corner of the seat, it is a fair indication that one is, in Western jargon, "a tenderfoot." Conversely a driver who sits "tall in the saddle," alert, head up, hands on the wheel, creates the impression that he knows what he is doing. At least it's apparent that he learned the first lesson of driving an automobile.

Robert Benoist, a great French Grand Prix driver of the 1920's and 1930's once said, "The stability of a car depends on the personal stability of the driver." Though Benoist referred to emotional as well as physical balance, his implication is that if the driver is not under control the automobile most likely will not be either.

The first step in driver control or stability is proper seating position. Unless a person is sitting alert and comfortable behind the wheel, he is handicapping himself from the start.

Driving should not be a chore. In fact, the operation of a modern automobile on the highways in a safe and sensible manner can be decidedly pleasurable. The solution of highway situations and the control of horsepower with maximum efficiency can be a wonderfully stimulating activity.

Obviously a driver can never reach this point if his basic form is bad, any more than a golfer can break 80 if he uses his club like a baseball bat. Form behind the wheel is extremely important and without it anyone aspiring to drive at his best might as well take a bus.

A driver should fit his car. When a person slides behind the wheel, his arms should be slightly bent, naturally falling on the rim in a "ten to two" position (on the basis of a clock face) or so his hands grip the rim at points just above the imaginary line that bisects the wheel horizontally. His feet should easily reach the pedals while his spine is braced firmly by the back of the seat.

Normally, routine adjustments have to be made with the seat to obtain a comfortable position. A short person might find that once the seat is far enough forward so he can reach the pedals, he is almost beneath the wheel, forced to peer up and over the dashboard. Often a pillow will correct the problem. In other instances a trip to a garage for modifications in the seat location is required. The important point is this: if you plan to drive a car regularly, be sure you fit. Nothing can place a more immediate handicap on a driver than poor position at the wheel.

Be sure the steering wheel is far enough away from your body so that your elbows are clear of your midriff. This will give your arms maximum freedom of movement without your having to shift hand position on the wheel. And, because your arm and shoulder muscles are more relaxed in this position, driving will be less fatiguing. On earlier cars, being close to the wheel provided more leverage, but steering con-

11

Rodger Ward in one of the normal driving positions. The hands are on the ten o'clock and two o'clock segments of the wheel and the arms are slightly bent. Note that the driver is far enough away from the wheel so that turning movements can be made without the elbows rubbing against the midriff. Of course, the seat belt is fastened at all times.

12

temporary automobiles is relatively effortless, permitting the driver to sit well back.

Hold the steering wheel, don't clutch it. Gripping the wheel as if it is some sort of mainspring that might uncoil can only lead to fatigue. Some observations made by Herman Lang, a great driver of the 1930's, come to mind in this regard: "I kept looking at Nuvolari [the Italian Tazio Nuvolari, considered by some to be the greatest race driver of all time], a small, slender man, and wondered how he managed to produce so much strength. Was it perhaps that I was making too big an effort which was not really necessary? Thinking back, I realized that I had been holding the wheel with a vice-grip. Today [1952] I need only half the muscular strength and when I get out of the car after a 300 mile race, only my dirty face shows it, otherwise there is no sign of fatigue."°

The same is true of the Indianapolis 500-mile race, where drivers race for nearly four hours in the seat of a powerful car totally lacking in the creature comforts of a passenger automobile. What is most important is that they have a solid, stable seat and are able to go about their business without the fear that fatigue from poor seating will reduce efficiency.

Fatigue comes quickly when muscles are taut, so every effort must be made to remain physically relaxed (while keeping mentally alert).

Never use a smaller muscle if a larger one is avail-

° *Grand Prix Driver.* G. T. Foulis & Co. Ltd. 1952.

able. Use both arms to turn the wheel, don't tug with
one while letting the other take a free ride. If you sit
properly behind the wheel, with your hands in the
approved position, you will notice that directional
changes can be made by merely shifting your body
from side to side. Take advantage of this, using the
shoulders and body to supplement your arms. Of
course don't exaggerate this to a point where you're
"leaning" into a corner like a jockey.

Keep your head up. Aside from the obvious benefit
of increased visibility, this is less fatiguing. When your
head is drooped forward or tilted back, the neck and
shoulder muscles are operating at a decided mechanical disadvantage. And, believe it or not, your eyeball
muscles are at full stretch when your head is either
way forward or back. Strange as it sounds, this can
lead to weary eyes on long trips.

No matter how ideal your driving position might
be, it can become tiring after lengthy stints on the
highway. Measures for counteracting this difficulty
will be discussed at greater length in a later chapter,
but with reference to hand positions on the wheel a
simple corrective step can be taken. Try placing your
hands in a "twenty to four" position for a while. Holding the wheel below the imaginary bisecting line we
mentioned earlier, your palms will be in an upward
position, permitting the inside muscles of the arms to
take over a greater share of the work.

Oftentimes a driver will begin a trip sitting upright,

with his back properly supported, then slowly droop farther and farther down in the seat as he proceeds, all the while becoming less in control of his car. On other occasions he will slide slightly in his seat while rounding a corner and complete the trip sitting off center. Sometimes a driver can shift enough so that his vision in the rear-view mirror will be limited (provided he does not readjust it) and his application of the pedals can be hampered. These are seemingly minor points, but they may add up to serious mistakes on the road.

Aside from its unquestionable benefits as a safety device, a seat belt can be a great aid to driver stability. A belt tends to keep you in position, preventing you from slouching or sliding.

A real revelation comes to many drivers using a seat belt for the first time when they discover how much easier it is to stay behind the wheel. It is an unconscious reaction, but every driver is exerting a fair amount of energy to maintain his position when he rounds a curve or corner. With a belt holding you in place, that effort is unnecessary. A bucket seat will do the same thing, though it does not have the safety features of a seat belt.

Some people object to belts, arguing that with one on they can't move around in the seat. Well, they probably are forced to wiggle around in the seat because they're slouching and almost any position is uncomfortable. Anyway, a seat belt shouldn't be a tourniquet; a driver is permitted some movement with the belt in place.

We'll say it now and we'll say it many more times before the end of this book: Use a seat belt; it will add to your competency, your safety and your comfort behind the wheel.

It is one thing to hold the wheel right; it is another to turn it correctly. For straight-line travel the "ten to two" position provides the driver with the best way to make corrections to both the right and left. But more arm and hand movement is generally needed in a genuine corner. When entering a corner, hand position should be altered slightly. For example, if a right-hand bend is coming up, the driver should drop his right hand to the four-o'clock position on the wheel, thus placing his hands at 180 degrees from each other. This makes him ready to apply more steering lock (amount wheel is turned) should the turn decrease in radius or the car begin to understeer heavily (see Chapter 7). He is also in position to decrease lock as the turn straightens out or to correct should a patch of slippery surface begin a skid.

Technique varies for negotiating slow corners where more than one revolution of the wheel is required. Some experts counsel that hands should never be crossed on the wheel (when one hand moves from the bottom of the wheel to the top while the other continues the turning). They warn that this might cause the hands and arms to become tangled should an emergency arise. Others say this technique is the most natural and therefore the best. This should be up to the individual driver; turn tight corners in a way that feels most natural to you, remembering these three rules: (1) try to keep both hands on the wheel as much as possible during the turning sequence, (2) attempt to keep your hands on the opposite sides of the wheel for maximum control and leverage, and (3) never take both hands off the wheel; for example, while letting the natural caster action of the front wheels "spin" the car back on course.

No matter how ideal one's form, it will be a worthless asset unless it can be used to improve overall driving ability. Merely posing at the wheel in the accepted posture is not enough. The driver must feel comfortable and well acquainted with his surroundings.

A top-notch driver is aware of the location and the manner of operation of all the instruments in the automobile he is driving. He is able to snap on the lights, windshield wipers or other instruments without taking his eyes off the road; he knows how to read his gauges quickly and checks them periodically while under way.

Like a pilot, a driver should be "checked out" with his automobile before he gets on the highway. You can imagine how absurd it would be if a pilot had to search through the maze of instruments in front of him every time he wanted to check the altimeter. The same is true of the driver who gropes around for his

17

gas gauge. Time spent looking for a dial or a button means time spent with your eyes off the road, and few things can be more dangerous.

When a good aviator prepares for takeoff, he runs through a list of required operations, turning knobs and flicking switches in an orderly sequence. Though the job is considerably more complicated in an airplane, the highway driver should have his own little checkoff list before getting started.

Once the engine is running, the ammeter and oil pressure gauges (or warning lights) should be checked to be sure no malfunctions exist. The rear-view mirror should be adjusted and the seat moved to provide the best driving position. The brakes should be pumped once or twice to assure that they are in working order. If the drive is starting at night, the lights should be on and in the desired high or low beam. Generally the final movement before engaging the automobile in gear and starting off is the release of the parking brake. There is no excuse for having to wiggle the rear-view mirror into adjustment while driving along or discovering at the end of the driveway or at the first intersection that the brakes have lost their fluid.

By readying himself and his car, the driver will be subconsciously better prepared to drive.

When an expert climbs into a strange car for the first time, he takes care to learn the whereabouts of the various controls. If you drive a different car, run a "cockpit checkoff" before you get started.

Once on the road, check the instrument panel once every few minutes. (Let common sense be your guide; for example, don't try it when rounding a curve, approaching an intersection, etc.) With the contemporary warning lights for low oil pressure and battery discharge, a mere glance will tell you if everything is normal. Naturally a check of the fuel gauge is not necessary at such short intervals. The driver should have a fair idea how full his tank is without having to refer to the gauge constantly.

There are those people who overdo speedometer reading. Some motor along with one eye literally locked on the indicator needle. This of course is not safe—and yet erratic speed is not safe either. With experience comes a certain feel for speed. Drivers with years of highway time can tell their velocity within a few mph without constantly referring to the speedometer. Until that point is reached, keep track of your speed as often as you feel necessary. What is crucial is that you be familiar with the markings of the speedometer so that your eyes don't dally on the needle trying to determine what the actual speed is.

One final word on speedometer reading: With the power and silence of some modern cars, speed can build up to fairly impressive rates before you realize it. If you find a pattern developing where every time you look at the needle you are going faster than you think, *check* more often. A driver who is not aware that his speed is steadily increasing is headed for danger.

And there are few weaker excuses than, "Honest, officer, I didn't realize how fast I was going."

The smart, safe driver tries to stay ahead of the game at all times. He projects his thoughts to a point where he can ready himself for dangerous situations *before* they arrive. When he spots a car at the side of the road, he immediately begins to mentally thumb through the various evasive tactics he might take should that car do the abnormal or the unexpected. As he enters a curve he is prepared, at least subconsciously, for a patch of oil or ice. And when he pops over the brow of a hill his mind and body are ready for action should a car be passing in his lane or a cow be wandering in the road.

It would be wise for every driver to borrow the motto of the Boy Scouts. By being prepared, i.e., sitting tall and steady behind the wheel, being aware of the mechanical condition of the automobile, with a clear image of the traffic situation ahead and behind, you will be taking the first important step toward becoming a safe, proficient driver.

3

A SAFE AUTOMOBILE:
AN ESSENTIAL

A driver is only as safe as the automobile he is driving. Too often the entire responsibility for safe driving is placed on the shoulders of the driver. This is an oversimplification. Driving ability and saintly intentions cannot alone keep an automobile out of trouble. Obviously proper technique and manners behind the wheel are essential, but if the steering wheel wobbles uncertainly because the front suspension is out of alignment or pulls each time the brakes are applied, the driver's best efforts are useless.

Keeping his car in perfect repair should be the primary aim of every good driver. The automobile should be considered a tool and, like any other craftsman, the driver should do his best to keep it in excellent working condition.

The increasing highway speeds and the multiplying throngs of cars are steadily making all traffic situations more challenging. There is no place for the jalopy. Years ago, ownership of an old car slung together with the proverbial baling wire was a standard American joke. Under today's rugged driving conditions the jalopy is an American nightmare.

Insurance statistics trace only a small percentage

of automobile accidents to mechanical failure. But these figures are deceiving. They refer only to the outright breakdown, i.e., complete loss of steering or brakes, the shedding of a wheel, etc. Not included are the accidents caused (or at least assisted) by *inefficient* mechanical components. For example, take the driver who smashes into the rear of an automobile stopped at an intersection. His brake linings may have been worn down to shiny metal, cutting his stopping efficiency in half, but, as long as the brakes operated, the accident will not be reflected in the "mechanical failure" statistics.

We feel that a frightening percentage of accidents on the highways could be eliminated if all automobiles operated at their best. When viewed in this light, mechanical upkeep becomes an essential facet of good driving.

When speaking of car upkeep, American motorists can be divided into three general categories. Probably a majority fit into the group which sincerely try to keep their cars in good working order. But oftentimes they are motivated not by a desire to promote safe driving but by a desire to keep repair bills down. Unfortunately too many of them limit maintenance to punctual oil changes and the prompt elimination of annoying rattles. A lack of knowledge concerning what should be done to keep their automobiles in good repair oftentimes hampers this group.

Then there are those who drive an automobile until

it stops. Amazingly enough, this includes the owners of many new cars. Not a few will motor nonchalantly along, stopping only to fill the tank and adding oil only when a horrified gas station attendant shows them a bone-dry dipstick. Of course this group is the most hazardous on the highway. They are not in contact with their automobiles, and this lack of communication sometimes manifests itself in rude and sloppy tactics on the road. It might be generalized that the driver who treats his car with respect is a considerably safer and more proficient driver than the man who flogs his machine around like an indestructible beast of burden. Mechanical negligence is driving negligence and the teetotaler who drives without proper brakes or lights can cause just as horrendous an accident as the bleary-eyed drunk.

In the third group are the drivers who pay strict attention to the mechanical well-being of their automobiles. These people adhere to the concept of preventive maintenance; running gear is checked periodically and parts are oftentimes replaced before they start to show signs of heavy wear. In short, the automobile is treated as it should be, as a highly complicated device that requires steady care. This is not to imply that the contemporary car is frail. It is, considering the sophistication of some of its components, extremely rugged. But it will wear out. And without maintenance its useful life can be cut in half.

"What more can I do?" you may plead. "I change

the oil regularly and the car is washed and waxed every weekend." Of course these are desirable facets of automobile maintenance. But a brilliant paint job and a clean crankcase leave a car far below the optimum of safety.

Certainly the basis of a well-maintained car is a well-tuned engine. Without an engine that operates at full efficiency, an automobile is a hazard on the highway and a source of despair for its driver. To be safe in all driving conditions, an automobile must respond when the throttle is opened. There are many occasions on the road, especially during passing situations and at intersections, when a sputtering engine can be genuinely dangerous. At its best it will be hard on fuel and its reliability will be uncertain. The driver of an automobile with an untuned engine (and by "tuned" we don't mean an engine that will provide stunning acceleration and performance—a 30-hp European light sedan can be as well "tuned" as a 300-hp hardtop) is a dangerous individual on the road.

One doesn't have to be a graduate mechanical engineer to keep an automobile running efficiently. In fact, you don't have to know a socket wrench from a screwdriver. Literally thousands of mechanics are awaiting the opportunity to carry out this function. And every driver owes it to himself, his family, and his automobile to see that they get that chance.

Let your mechanic check the spark plugs every few thousand miles. They will last longer if they can be gapped periodically, and a check of this sort will reveal any malfunctions in the carburetors that may lead to poor gas mileage and impeded performance.

The ignition points should be adjusted at regular intervals. When these contacts, which transmit the electric current to the spark plugs, become a few thousandths of an inch out of position, they burn out quickly and mileage and performance again suffer.

The ignition system has been called the heart of an engine. As a rule, good mechanics will trace poor performance to the ignition system while others fiddle with the carburetors, fuel pump, etc. If points and plugs are clean and gapped, if the engine's timing is on the mark, if the wiring is in good repair and if the battery and generator are functioning as they should be, the driver has taken a big step toward making his automobile safe.

This is not to say that other segments of the engine need no attention. Be sure that the radiator hoses and all the drive belts for the fan, generator, etc., are in good condition. Make sure cylinder head and valve cover gaskets don't leak.

One normally ignored step toward safe engine performance is cleanliness. Look under the hood of a top-notch racing car and you will find a spotless engine compartment. Then check the engine of the next car you see broken down beside the road. Chances are it's covered with a massive layer of grease, mud and rust. Smart mechanics don't keep their engines clean merely to satisfy their urge for sanitation. Practically speaking, a clean engine is easier to work on and trouble is much easier to spot if it isn't concealed beneath two inches of grease or in a rat's nest of wiring. If your engine is in this condition, a few dollars for a steam-cleaning job would be money well spent.

Strong, reliable brakes are an absolute necessity. Any pull or fade that decreases stopping efficiency is just as hazardous as the braking system that stops operating entirely. In fact, the outright failure might be better in some instances. At least the driver, if he is fortunate enough to get his automobile stopped without hitting anything, will be forced to get the brakes repaired. But the man with inadequate brakes will drive casually onward, oftentimes stopping only after his car has planted itself against some unyielding object.

The ironic thing about good brakes is that they are relatively simple to maintain. Brake linings are tough and will provide dependable service for many thousands of miles. There are few moving parts in the system and any good mechanic can keep it in working order for next to nothing.

Your foot will tell you a great deal about your brakes. If the pedal gets more than a few inches of play or free action, then they should be adjusted. If the pedal feels spongy and the brakes don't seem to take a firm bite, chances are air has gotten into the hydraulic lines and will have to be "bled" out. This is a simple operation that can be performed at any gas station.

On occasion brakes will get out of adjustment to a point where the automobile will pull to one side or the other when stopping. The dangerous part of this ailment is that it may never make itself apparent until heavy applications of the brakes are made. In other words, the brakes may appear to work fine when one is coasting up to a stop sign, but a hard punch on the pedal at 60 mph may literally yank the car off the road.

This is a condition that may creep up on the driver who uses his automobile steadily in slow traffic conditions or in gentle grocery-store tripping. After never calling upon his brakes at high speeds, he ventures out onto the open road for a long trip and finds that he might as well have dragged his feet when slowing from higher velocities.

Before a race car is cleared for competition in the Indianapolis 500 and in all road-racing events, it must undergo a brake test. And that test, both simple and safe, should be undertaken periodically by every driver on the road.

This is how it works: At 10–15 mph, depending on space, take your hands off the steering wheel and jam the breaks on—hard. Have someone standing by the car to watch the action of the wheels. If a wheel locks up and skids while the others continue to roll, the brakes need adjustment. If they squeal, the linings may be worn to a point where they need replacement. Don't forget that the malfunctions that make themselves apparent in this little test will multiply themselves tremendously as the speed increases.

In many cases, your driveway will have adequate room for this experiment. Of course don't try it at too fast a speed or where you might run into something.

A good general rule is to have the brake drums removed and checked every 10,000 miles after the initial 20,000 miles. A mechanic can pull a brake drum in a matter of minutes, and a quick check of the condition of the shoes, the rubber seals on the wheel cylinders of the hydraulic system and the drums can be made. Normally, because a heavy percentage of the braking is absorbed by the front pair, a check of one of the two forward wheels should reveal any serious malfunctions. Also make a habit of having the level of the hydraulic brake fluid reservoir checked at lubrication intervals. Any leaks in the system will rapidly deplete the fluid, leaving you dependent on fervent prayer for stopping power.

In the past decade, gigantic strides have been made by the rubber industry to make tires tougher and safer. Whereas the blowout was once the bugaboo of all drivers, modern tubeless tires have all but eliminated that danger. In fact, the situation might appear a little too rosy for the driving public's own good. Many people now seem to feel that tires are so husky that normal maintenance is not necessary. This is ridiculous. In the first place, proper care will add thousands of miles to the life of the tires and, secondly, few things can make an automobile less safe than badly worn rubber. Today's tires are generally extremely safe from blowouts caused by punctures, but no manufacturer's warranty will stand behind a tire that is worn smooth. When a tire reaches this stage, it is just as prone to failure as the models of thirty years ago.

The primary step in accepted tire care is the maintenance of air pressure. If the tires on your automobile are inflated correctly, the rubber will wear evenly and the car will handle better. As a standard rule, keep about 30 pounds of air in the tires. This will reduce the ultra-smooth ride slightly and may make the tires a bit more noisy, but the radical improvement in handling will more than offset these drawbacks. Additionally, sidewall flex (while turning, the sidewalls of the tires tend to buckle under the weight of the automobile) is cut down and the tires should wear longer. Try to make a habit of checking air pressure every week or so, whether the car is driven or not. And remember, check the tires when they are cool, because when they are warm the air inside expands and pressure readings taken under these conditions will be deceivingly high.

Front wheel alignment is an absolute necessity in keeping tires safe. When the "front end," as the forward suspension is called, is out of alignment, one or both of the front tires is not rolling flat and true over the road surface. Under these conditions, with the tires scuffing along the highway, rubber mileage nose-dives. If the steering of your car tends to pull in one direction or the other, chances are the front end is in need of alignment. If this is the case, have it corrected immediately by a professional.

Unbalanced wheels (including the tires) can raise Cain with tire mileage. In this situation, one or more segments of the wheel are heavier than the rest, caus-ing it to undulate as it rolls along. At low speeds poor balance is hardly a factor, but when velocities reach a point where centrifugal force around the perimeter of the tire is very strong, real trouble begins. At certain speeds this condition will reveal itself in the form of severe vibrations. Normally these critical speeds will be somewhere between 40 and 60 mph. The driver will find that the condition will disappear if he reduces or increases speed. If this condition ap-pears, don't go faster. Though the vibration may seem to stop, the unbalance is still there and tire wear and the chance of tire failure multiply to an alarming degree. There is only one way to correct improper wheel balance: most service stations and tire shops have equipment to rectify this situation and it should be done immediately when the trouble is detected.

Though few drivers realize it, they negotiate left-hand corners faster than right handers. This is probably because, with our left-hand steering, they have a better view of a corner on that side and therefore motor through a bit more boldly. Because weight transfers to the outside of the car in a corner, the right tires will normally wear faster than the left. Add to this the increased scuffing the right tires get against curbs and the fact that tires on this side run more frequently on the abrasive stones and gravel on the edge of the road and it becomes apparent that rubber on the right tires will disappear faster.

Herein lies the reason for rotating the tires. By switching the rubber periodically, drivers will get even wear from all five (including the spare). The chart below indicates the most satisfactory method of making this rotation.

A driver does not have to be a tire expert to determine how his tires are wearing. A sight inspection will reveal if the tread is wearing off one section of

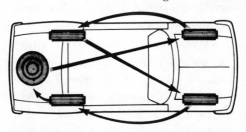

One of several accepted ways of rotating tires. The system shown here is recommended because it utilizes all five tires carried on the automobile, including the spare. Whatever pattern is selected for switching the tires, it should always be followed consistently. In other words, once you begin using a certain tire-rotation plan, stick to it to insure even wear.

the tire faster than another. Running one's fingertips over the tread surface will also help; if one row of tread feels higher than another, chances are the tire is wearing unevenly. If you are in doubt, take the automobile to a service station for a definite answer. Smart drivers will normally have their tires inspected every 5,000 miles and prior to every major trip.

Shock absorbers are commonly thought to be relatively unimportant little devices that do nothing more than smooth out unpleasant bumps in the highway. Actually they are crucial to proper control of an automobile. Heavy leaning on corners, excessive nosedive while stopping, steering vibrations and a tendency for an automobile to float and wander down the road are the hazards of poor shock absorbers.

Essentially, shock absorbers keep the wheels on the ground. If the springing action was permitted to run free, the wheels would bounce happily into the air on each bump. Likewise, in cornering, the weight transfer we mentioned earlier tends to lift weight from the inside wheels and place it on the outside pair. With the wheels off the ground or at a point where they are not exerting maximum bite on the road surface, traction is lost and control suffers. By dampening this springing action, shock absorbers are the real key to stability in your automobile.

If your shocks are in good working order, you can shove down hard on the front or rear fenders and the suspension will return quickly and firmly to position.

When the shock absorbers are worn out, the springs will bounce several times before coming to rest.

We recommend a slightly stiffer shock than normal for increased stability and control, especially if you tow a trailer or load your car heavily. Like higher tire pressures, this will slightly reduce that "Cloud Nine" ride many drivers look for, but the less resilient suspension will make the automobile much safer and certainly more satisfying to drive.

A good driver should prefer top-notch handling to a soft ride. And, surprisingly enough, the slightly firmer ride inherent in stiffer shocks is less fatiguing. First of all, the driver has to exert less effort in controlling the automobile and, secondly, a mushy, bouncy ride causes the human body to make continuous, unconscious muscular adjustments that are extremely tiring.

The important thing to remember about shock absorbers is that they will wear out. No matter how docilely an automobile is driven, it should not be expected that the shocks will last more than two years or 25,000 miles. If a car is driven with more than normal enthusiasm, or on consistently rough roads, they may wear out within 10,000 or 15,000 miles. If your shock absorbers get weak and sloppy, replace them; you will be a better driver for it.

Weather conditions can have a definite bearing on the mechanical capabilities of your automobile. For example, if you live on the seacoast and drive into the mountains, the decreased atmospheric pressure (which forces the fuel mixture of gasoline and air into the carburetors) will force the engine to run too rich, or on too much gasoline in proportion to air. This is nothing that will spell outright disaster, but it must be considered when passing or climbing hills because performance will definitely be reduced. Of course the situation can easily be corrected by having the carburetors readjusted when you reach the mountains. (If this is done, don't forget to reset them once again when you return to the lowlands.)

You may notice that your automobile's engine will seem to run better in the early-morning hours before dawn or when the weather is overcast. This is a matter of air density. During these periods the moisture content of the air is high and the engine will show a slight boost in performance.

On the debit side of the ledger, rain and morning dampness will oftentimes cause brakes to grab unevenly. How this can be overcome will be discussed further in Chapter 6.

Cold, dry weather, with the thermometer hovering well below freezing, may slow your car down. Throttle response may be reduced, meaning the engine will cough for more fuel before catching hold. This is caused by the air being so dense that the engine tends to run "lean" or with an overbalance of air-to-gasoline mixture. If the automobile is equipped with a choke, this situation may be overcome; but to avoid trouble when the weather is like this, the driver should still judge his driving so that he will not have to call on great bursts of acceleration.

It shouldn't even be necessary to make mention of the fact that all lights should be in working order. Telling a driver to keep all his lights in proper repair is like telling him he should have tires on all his wheels; if he isn't aware of the fact, he shouldn't be driving. However, weather can have a decided effect on lighting efficiency. Snow and ice will often form on headlights to a point where their range can be cut nearly in half. This may happen so gradually that a driver will not be aware of the reduction. While this is happening up front, the tail lights may become completely obscured. When driving in sleet and wet snow or on muddy surfaces keep this in mind and stop occasionally to clean off the lenses.

During the summer months insects and dirt may lodge against the headlight lenses to a point where candlepower may be seriously reduced. Therefore it's a good idea before you drive at night to wipe the lights clean, be it summer or winter. The vibration of normal driving will, in time, knock headlights out of adjustment. Again, this may happen so slowly that the driver will not be aware of the change. Have your headlights reset every 10,000 to 15,000 miles.

Probably one of the most distressing sights on the roads is an automobile decked out in regalia like mudflaps, gaudy wheel spinners, etc., while being in fact a mechanical nightmare. This is unfortunate because in most instances if half of the money spent on decorations had been directed toward repairs the automobile would have been worth something.

The sad part about this is that individuals in this category are generally referred to as hot rodders. This is a gross injustice to the true rodder of today. Generally responsible young men, the hot rodder's car is normally in excellent mechanical condition.

Rodders refer to the drivers of these dolled-up junkers or "gook wagons" as "shot rodders" or "chokes." If you are a young driver, be sure you don't fall into this group.

Of course, there's no law against decking out your automobile as you see fit, no matter how weird the result might be, but it is more important that the machine be mechanically perfect when you put it on the road.

There is a trend in most states with acute traffic problems toward periodic mechanical inspections for all automobiles. This is an outstanding idea and should provide tangible results in terms of lowered accident rates. If your state has such a plan, cooperate with the authorities; if such a policy is being discussed, give it your support.

Remember, an automobile is, outside of a home, the biggest single investment made in most people's lifetimes. Anything you can do to keep it in safe and sound condition makes you not only a better driver but a smarter businessman and a better citizen.

4

KNOW YOUR LIMITATIONS

Our way of life revolves around the concept that all men are created equal. But, contrary to what we might be inclined to believe, this applies only to social and political justice. Unfortunately not all of us possess identical physical and mental strength. Equality must be interpreted in terms of the opportunities, not the capabilities, of each individual. And on this basis, there is a very good chance that a substantial number of our fellow citizens are both stronger and smarter than we are.

Each individual must face up to his weaknesses and exploit his strengths. Take, for example, the tennis player whose serve and forehand have considerably less velocity than his opponent's. To counteract this disadvantage, he may concentrate on defensive ability and accuracy in his volleys. The same is true in driving; we must realize our weaknesses and drive accordingly. For example, a fair percentage of our citizens are color blind. To the smart driver this handicap means more caution at the intersection and a sharper than normal lookout on the road for danger markings. Depth perception and reflexes also vary greatly from individual to individual, as do vision, judgment, etc.

It doesn't take a complete examination by your family doctor to obtain a fair notion of your physical capabilities behind the wheel. Of course, determining the sharpness of your senses, like strength of vision and hearing ability, must be left up to your doctor. However, other important facets of your physical makeup can be tested in your own home.

Depth perception, the quality which permits the individual to judge the relative distance of objects ahead, can be tested by placing a pair of blocks (or toy cars, for realism) on a table or flat surface about three to five feet away. By use of strings attached to a third similar object, try to move it to a point exactly nose-to-nose with the other pair. If it can be positioned consistently within inches of the other two, the indication is that your depth perception is satisfactory. Conversely, if you find your calculations

Two simple tests for getting a better idea of your driving capabilities. The top drawing shows a model car on a string being maneuvered into position at eye level with the table. If you are able to position the model so that its bumper is within a few inches of the two cars flanking it, the chances are good that your depth perception is normal. If you miss the mark by more than a few inches, you should assume that your depth perception is not up to par and use extra caution when driving, especially in passing and braking.

The bottom picture shows a way to test peripheral vision. If your hand passes out of sight within the smaller of the two arcs, you must be especially careful about checking traffic when passing, turning, or entering an intersection, because your peripheral vision is below normal. If you can still see your hand when it is at right angles to your body (wider arc), then your side vision is normal.

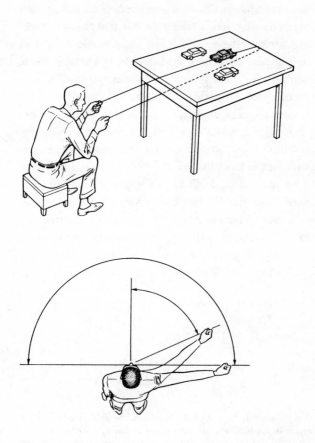

off, take account of this deficiency and profit by knowing about it: always give yourself an added margin in passing, never taking the risk that the approaching car may be too close; be extra cautious at dusk and in periods of poor visibility. In this way, you can compensate for a physical disadvantage—a disadvantage, incidentally, that cannot be overcome by all the desire, courage or experience in the world. If your depth perception is poor, face it and drive accordingly.

Ideally, you should be able to spread your arms straight out from the sides of your body and still keep your hands in sight. Chances are you will have to move your arms slightly forward before your hands come into view. This peripheral vision can be an extremely important factor in driving, especially in heavy traffic. Literally thousands of unnecessary accidents occur each year when someone whips out of a lane to pass

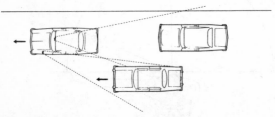

A side mirror is not a gadget. Note how the field of vision of the driver in the leading car is increased by his side mirror. Without this mirror it is possible that the passing car would approach unobserved. The "blind spot" in cars not equipped with side mirrors may conceal a full-sized automobile and has been the cause of any number of accidents.

and cuts smack into the path of an overtaking car. Some of these mishaps are caused by sheer neglect; the driver just didn't bother to look before he cut the wheel over. In other instances the driver actually looked before turning but just didn't see anything. Maybe lack of peripheral vision was at fault.

If you are forced to move your hands more than 20 degrees forward before they come into view, watch out on the highway because your peripheral vision is poor. If this is the case, make an effort to twist your head around to get a full view of the situation before pulling out. Better yet, install a healthy-sized side mirror on your car. This device, which some of our more austere citizens rank with fender skirts as a needless ornament, is recommended for every driver. A side mirror can be extremely valuable in keeping the driver informed of what is going on over his left shoulder, an area out of the visibility arc of the regular rear-vision mirror.

Without the help of a neurologist or a psychologist, it is rather hard to make an appraisal of your reflexes. And once evaluated, it is extremely difficult to correlate reflex action with capability behind the wheel. A person with excellent reflexes and a wandering mind or poor physical coordination can be a terrifyingly unsafe driver. A driver must be able to translate reflex action into correct physical action, i.e., stepping on the brakes or throttle, turning the wheel, etc. If this cannot be done, lightning reflexes are a questionable asset.

Young drivers are acknowledged to have quicker reflexes than their elders. Yet they have more than their share of accidents. Why? Because some of this group are confident their quick wits will get them out of any dangerous situation. This, coupled with a natural exuberance, causes some of them to overdrive. Under these circumstances they barrel into their first emergency situation like this: Their reflexes, honed to a sharp edge, recognize the difficulty immediately, and they set about grappling at the controls in a violent attempt to avoid the crash. Often they are so far over their heads speedwise when the trouble arises that a Stirling Moss could not prevent the accident. In other cases, the corrective action is in itself wrong and only makes a serious situation hopeless.

Reflexes are worthless in driving unless they are backed up with experience and discretion. For the most part, their role in highway driving has been exaggerated. A person does not have to have acute reflexes to drive well on the road. Of course they can be extremely valuable in certain situations if the alarm sound leads to the proper corrective action. Be thankful if you have quick reflexes, but don't depend on them.

Going beyond normal physical capabilities, the question of emotional adaptability to driving becomes more and more important each day. With higher speeds and heavier congestion on contemporary high-ways, mental stability is an absolute must. Remember once again the words of Robert Benoist: "The stability of a car depends on the personal stability of the driver." Are all drivers emotionally fit to handle an automobile? Before you decide, consider this: Several years ago a detailed psychiatric study was made on 10,000 drivers in a large Midwestern city. Of that total, more than 1,000 had had or needed psychiatric treatment. Nearly 100 more were literally mentally unbalanced and should have been in institutions!

Naturally statistics such as these point up the need for more rigid examinations to obtain a driver's license —and periodic retesting. Many people are in fine shape when they get their licenses and then continue to use the road despite the fact that they may have lost arms, legs, eyes or even their minds!

Though the vast majority of drivers on the road are what we would describe as normal individuals, mental attitude and stability are still important to them. Most people don't realize that their driving ability varies day by day in accordance with their general outlook on the world. Take the man who has a little spat with his wife just before he drives off to work. Or the person who is on his way to the funeral of a loved one. Certainly neither of these people could be described as being in a settled frame of mind. And this change from their normal attitude will affect their driving, as it will affect their behavior in every other facet of their

43

lives. The man who has had the quarrel may release his anger and frustration by driving more aggressively; the mourner may find that his grief has distracted him completely from his driving.

Add to this the daily changes in physical condition. Everything from a head cold to a hangnail can have an influence on a person's ability behind the wheel. Even minor ailments can deaden reflexes and cut efficiency.

Driving ability can vary from day to day, even from hour to hour. In most instances the variations will be so slight that overall safety is not impeded. But on those occasions when you feel different, either physically or mentally, adjust your driving accordingly. Generally speaking, the adjustment should come in terms of extra caution and reduced speed.

Because of this, beware of the driver who says, "I *always* drive 65 mph on the highway." This person is headed for trouble. Anyone who arbitrarily travels at a certain speed all the time is not compensating for changes in ability and is therefore overdriving on many occasions.

Always maintain what seems like a comfortable speed, never forcing yourself to go faster. If you have a headache or a bad cold, make a rule of slowing down because you are not as sharp as you think you are. Give yourself a chance.

Young men and women who are starting out today as drivers have some tremendous disadvantages to overcome with regard to learning their limitations. In the first place, the general enthusiasm of youth is by nature opposed to thinking in terms of limitations. No one likes to think of himself as limited in any way, least of all behind the wheel. Secondly, the cars we drive are so deceptively simple that it appears on the surface that anyone can learn to drive in a matter of moments. Of course this is not the case. Learning to operate properly a device commonly possessing over 200 hp and weighing over 1½ tons is a mighty big job for anyone.

Aim first for experience. You cannot be taught to handle an automobile; that can only come after a "feel" for the machine has been developed—and that in turn only comes after hours behind the wheel.

Teenage girls sometimes lack confidence in their driving while boys go to the other extreme, often driving completely beyond themselves. For the most part, boys have a better feeling for driving than girls. If they can be given a proper sense of prudence by the instructor, they should require less training time than their female counterparts. Some girls may need three or four times more instruction before their confidence reaches the right level.

Be you young or old, you have certain limitations as a driver. And those limitations are most certainly not determined by how close you can get the throttle to the firewall. Nor do they have any bearing on your bodily strength or your intelligence quotient. Some

highly intelligent people are abominable drivers because they can't keep their minds on the job at hand.
Stupid people are generally dangerous because they
lack judgment or discretion. Who then is a good
driver? It is the person who knows his limitations and
drives within them, a person who is responsible to
himself, his fellow drivers and to his automobile.

Psychological tests are now coming into use which
seemingly can sort out good drivers from bad merely
on the basis of how people answer certain questions.
If a young man indicates he would rather be a scout
master than a plumber, statistics seem to support the
fact that he will be a safer driver. Much of this sort
of testing is based on the relative aggressiveness of
people. Supposedly the less-aggressive individual is
less likely to be involved in accidents.

Such tests are valuable but should never be taken
as the last word in judging drivers. They only indicate attitude, not aptitude. In other words, testing
may reveal the persons who will and will not race
their automobiles down the road at 120 mph. The
person who engages in this sort of nonsense is most
certainly headed for trouble, but so may be the person
who expresses no interest in this activity. His deficiency may lie in a complete lack of ability to drive.

If a test indicates that you have a tendency toward
aggressiveness behind the wheel, take it in your stride.
Make a conscious effort to control it on the highway.
By the same token, if you appear, on the basis of your

test grade, to be wonderfully suited to driving, watch out too. You may not, by lack of ability or experience, be qualified to back down your driveway.

Skill behind the wheel is almost impossible to judge. In the first place, there are very few people discerning enough to sort the good drivers from the bad ones. Chances are only *you* will ever be able to judge your own driving. But if you approach the job with a clear idea of your physical limitations and with a sincere desire to drive every foot of highway just as well as you know how, you'll be off to a fine start.

5

GEAR CHANGING

From the moment Daimler, Ford and Selden began tinkering with their primitive cars, it was obvious that some sort of gearing was necessary for maximum efficiency. Without gears the engine is limited to one level of operation.

If the gearless engine is so set up that it will move smartly along a level stretch, it will lose power and finally lurch to a halt on the first steep hill. Conversely, if it is designed to climb hills easily, the car's speed will be seriously limited during flat running.

Simply speaking, gears are installed to change the mechanical advantage of the engine. Say we have a car with a single gear ratio of 1:1, meaning the wheels make one revolution each time the crankshaft of the engine makes a revolution. With this system the engine will move the automobile along in fine fashion at a constant speed. However, the setup makes it hard for the engine to overcome any resistance. For that matter, starting from a dead stop would be extremely difficult.

To give the engine a better chance, let's install a gear behind the engine. By means of a control linkage from the driver's seat, the gear can be engaged and disengaged from the drive line, or the line which carries power from the engine to the driving wheels.

The gear will have a ratio of 16:1, meaning that the engine will (disregarding, for the sake of simplicity, the differential gears at the rear) turn 16 times faster than the rear wheels. Of course, with this mechanical advantage, the engine has a good bit more power but, because it can operate just so fast, the overall speed of the car is much less than with the original 1:1 ratio.

Now a device called a clutch, which will cut the power between the engine and transmission, permits us to select either our 16:1 ratio or our 1:1 ratio, depending on whether driving conditions demand power or speed.

The ratio of 16:1 (or let's call it "first" gear) will permit a maximum speed of 20 mph. At the same time the car has to be moving at 40 mph before the 1:1 ratio (or "second") will work efficiently. What is needed is another gear to provide a step between the two. This gear will, with a ratio of say 8:1, become "second" while our original 1:1 ratio moves up to "third."

What we have now are three gear ratios for three speed and power ranges. First gear for starting and climbing steep hills, second gear for acceleration and intermediate hills and third gear for high-speed travel at steady speeds on level ground. Each gear has specific advantages and limitations: first gear—power

49

but no speed; second gear—a compromise, some power, some speed; and third gear—speed but no power.

Early cars had basic transmissions of this sort. Because of their lack of mechanical refinement, the ratios were poorly spaced and most were perfect misery to get in and out of gear. Up until the 1930's a fair amount of experience and dexterity was required to engage a transmission smoothly, escaping the telltale crunching of protesting gears.

Then came the wonderful synchromesh gearboxes which permitted even the rankest novice to make gear changes without that embarrassing grinding. But even then poorly timed shifts could make the automobile buck or stall.

Automatic transmissions came on the scene in quantity following World War II. Suddenly the woes of gear changing disappeared, now handled completely by a little box full of gears and hydraulic fluid. All one had to do to make the car move was to slip a selector arm into the desired notch and step on the gas. From there on everything was cared for by that churning box that carried a variety of names like "Dynaflow," "Powerglide," "Cruise-O-Matic" and "Torque-Flite."

Designers have been working with the idea since the turn of the century, and the perfected systems of today can be operated by almost anyone, are relatively inexpensive to purchase and plenty reliable. Since

1954 a heavy percentage of cars manufactured in the United States have featured automatic transmissions.

Recently, for a number of reasons involving the influence of European cars and a more frugal attitude on the part of American consumers, the swing is reversing somewhat toward standard or "stick" shift gearboxes.

Actually it is difficult to make a choice between contemporary automatic and standard transmissions. Both are extremely smooth and silent to use. What advantages the automatic has in simplicity of operation are equaled by the greater flexibility of today's three- and four-speed all-synchromesh transmissions.

Both have their disadvantages; the automatic version generally gives poorer gas mileage because of slippage within the fluid coupling, is more expensive to purchase and repair and does not leave the selection of the exact gear up to the driver. The standard transmission automobile is harder to operate, takes more effort on the part of the driver and may suffer more readily from misuse (although both types are very rugged).

Whichever system is chosen by the driver, there is decidedly a right and wrong way of operation, even in the case of the super-simple automatic, where seemingly the whole process has been reduced to fingertip actuations of levers or buttons.

All contemporary automatics are so devised that the engine cannot be started while the transmission is in

Drive or, in other words, when the car is ready to move. The reason for this is obvious. Without such a provision, the automobile would leap ahead the moment the starter kicked over.

Once the engine is properly warmed up and you are ready to get under way, be sure to apply the brake as you move the selector arm into Drive. This will prevent the automobile from jumping off the mark once the transmission is engaged. If the unit is operating correctly, this should not happen, but if the engine is idling too fast or the automatic choke is not functioning properly, the car may creep as soon as the shift into Drive is made. Holding the automobile with the foot brake is also easier on the works. If the machine is inclined to creep, it will probably begin moving before the transmission is completely engaged. This will mean the Drive or Reverse (depending on which way you're heading) will take hold with a nasty "clunk." That noise means things are not engaging smoothly in the transmission and this usually can be avoided by using the brake.

If your automobile tends to creep, use the foot brake at stoplights or while momentarily halted in traffic. It is not a good idea to shift into Neutral on these occasions. A fair number of accidents have occurred when the driver, after seeing the light turn green, hurriedly snapped the selector arm into what he thought was Drive and then backed smartly into the car behind him. In his haste to get under way he picked the Reverse slot rather than Drive. Stay in gear in traffic.

Most automatic transmissions are equipped with a Low gear for special uses. This was *not* installed to assure the driver respectable results in the "stoplight grand prix." Low gear or Low range should be used primarily on hills, both in ascent and descent. More power will be provided for climbing (just like first gear in our simple gearbox) with Low range when going up and, surprisingly enough, it will be of real benefit on the way down. By utilizing what is called engine braking, a lower gear (in both standard and automatic transmissions) can be extremely valuable as a speed-checking mechanism. As you remember, a lower gear permits the engine to operate at a higher rpm than the driving wheels. When going downhill, the compression of the engine can be used as a brake. Because more compression strokes (the sequence of a four-cycle gasoline engine: intake, compression, ignition, exhaust) come when the engine is operating at a higher speed, engine braking is more powerful in a lower gear. As an indication of this, take your automobile out on a side road and run it at 25 mph in low gear, then take your foot off the throttle and see how quickly speed drops off. Now go the same speed in top gear and release the throttle. Notice how much less deceleration results. By dropping into Low range on very steep descents you can keep the speed of your automobile at a sensible level without overusing your brakes.

Of course common sense must be your guide as to when to engage Low gear in hilly country. Obviously it should not be used on every incline. If you expect to exceed the normal speed limit of Low in your car (generally between 40 and 50 mph) on the way down, stay in Drive. You cannot expect to drop into Low at speeds above its rpm limit. This causes excessive revving, which leads to all sorts of difficulties up to and including "blowing" the engine.

A refinement of the automatic transmission is the dual-range unit. This gives the driver double the number of speed ranges. For example, he can use Low-range Drive for brisk acceleration in traffic and High-range Drive for open-road travel. High-range Low can be employed on moderately steep hills, while Low-range Low is useful for ultra-steep inclines or perhaps for towing.

One more word of caution: Don't use the Low-to-Drive upshift technique (with a wide-open throttle) for maximum "dig" away from the lights. Most automatic transmissions are not built for this sort of monkey business and the abuse can mean staggering repair bills. Certainly that gain of a half second won't do you any good when you're being towed home with a shattered transmission.

The same engine-braking procedure mentioned for use on hills can be helpful on slippery pavement.

Because of the weight transfer to the front of an automobile while stopping, the forward brakes will often lock up tight when applied on icy, snowy or wet surfaces. Though we will pursue the question of braking in detail in the following chapter, let it be said for now that locked-up wheels are nearly useless for stopping. The wheels will continue to turn as the automobile slows in a low gear or Low range, making this a fine technique for use on poor-adhesion pavements.

However, if you are driving along and suddenly roar onto a patch of wet or icy road, *don't* pop into a lower range. This sudden deceleration will have the same effect as braking and could very well send the car spinning off the road.

For those who become stuck in mud or snow, there is a system called "rocking" that may help. Alternating directions forward, back, forward, back causes a rapid weight transfer which may extract the automobile. On the surface it would appear to be a simple trick with an automatic transmission—just alternating from Low to Reverse. Essentially this is correct, but a great deal of finesse is necessary in rocking, both to get the car out and to save the transmission. Tread *lightly* on the throttle for two reasons; one, spinning wheels have no traction, and two, you can imagine the convulsions the transmission and rear end would be going through in switching directions every few seconds at full throttle! When rocking with an automatic unit, treat the automobile gently, only applying throttle when one or the other gear is engaged and releasing the gas while shifting. (More on rocking in Chapter 11.)

With a little common sense, almost anyone can operate an automatic transmission automobile efficiently. The same is not true with a standard or "stick" shift. A fair amount of experience is needed before the driver can get the feel of engaging the clutch and gears smoothly and get his hand and foot movements down to a point where he is pushing and pulling at the right moment.

Like most operations requiring bodily coordination, manual gear changing cannot be learned from a book. Tips can be offered and refinements suggested, but the basic operation must be learned behind the wheel. And, to be a really good driver, it *must* be learned. Of course a person can go through life with a series of automatic transmission cars, never so much as touching a clutch pedal, but he will be lacking one of the most basic skills of driving.

Learning to operate a manual transmission gives the driver a feel of the machine that never comes with the automatic systems. Because he is more responsible for the performance of the automobile through the selection of the proper gear, a much stronger link exists between car and driver. The driver soon develops a feel for automobiles that he will never develop by using the other system. Gear changing is one of the real essentials of driving and no one should think of himself as a first-class motorist before he has become completely familiar with the "box," as the manual transmission is sometimes called. By providing a better sense of what's going on mechanically, manual shift experience will help you operate an automatic transmission better. But if you have learned with an automatic, don't expect it to help you a bit with manual shifting.

Simply speaking, a manual gear change is made when the clutch is depressed and the shifting mechanism is moved from one gear to another. Then, when the clutch is released, the power is transmitted through the gear which was just selected.

Timing the change so that engine speed roughly matches gear speed is the secret to making silky-smooth shifts. If the engine is running too slowly when the clutch is let out, the automobile will buck like a steer. And an engine running too rapidly will cause the car to jerk ahead.

You must gain this sense of engine speed–car speed equalization on the highway. It cannot be taught here, though one simple note might be made: When changing up (from first to second or from second to third), don't take your foot completely off the throttle. In other words, back off but keep a little power on. You will have to make adjustments in the amount of throttle you use and that, surprisingly enough, will come very easily.

A driver must not only concern himself with how

to shift but *when* to shift. As you remember, each gear has a specific mission and its use is appropriate only in certain situations. Unless you have this sense of when to use a gear, the whole concept of proper gearbox usage will escape you.

Take a driver who is just getting under way from a stoplight. He may take the car to 15–20 mph in first gear. At this point the limit of the efficient operating range of first gear is being reached and the driver changes up to second gear. He may let his speed climb to 25–35 mph in second gear before changing into third. Of course if he were attempting to obtain maximum acceleration, he might remain in first gear until 30 mph was reached and until he hit 55–70 mph in second (entirely dependent on the gearing of his car). Likewise if he were climbing a steep hill, he might not change to second as he reached 20 mph, knowing full well that he needed the power of first gear to pull him up.

Generally speaking, routine driving conditions dictate that 15 mph in first and 30 mph in second are sensible shifting points. Naturally this is flexible and will vary from car to car. You will have to determine for yourself exactly where the best points to shift are in your automobile.

If the engine begins to rev higher than normal and acceleration begins to drop off, you will have passed the most efficient shifting point. Conversely, if the engine hammers and snorts or will not pick up speed smoothly, you will know that you have shifted too early.

Don't shift according to time intervals. Some people who consider themselves quite capable drivers shift on the weird basis of *time* in each gear. They start out, drive, say, three seconds in first and five seconds in second before shifting. This is ridiculous. You can imagine the results if going up a hill. The poor engine would be straining its insides out because the shifts were made too early. And on the way down a hill the engine would probably overrev because each gear was used too long. Govern your shifting by the requirements of the road conditions, *not ever* on the basis of time.

Lazy drivers will sometimes skip second gear. In our contemporary automobiles power is such that they will accelerate in satisfactory fashion without using second gear. But the practice is not recommended. Three gears were installed and all three should be used. Only in this way will the automobile operate at maximum efficiency. The "second gear skipper" may not realize it, but his car's acceleration may drop off radically when he pops from first to third. This may hold up traffic behind him until he gets moving again. It's one of those habits in driving that you might get away with for fifty years without any trouble, but it is a sloppy and sometimes inconsiderate technique.

Though few people realize it, a great deal of wear can be caused by keeping the clutch disengaged for long periods of time. Don't wait in traffic for more than a minute with the clutch depressed. If you expect to be stopped for longer durations, slip the transmission into neutral and let out the clutch.

In the same vein, *never* hold your automobile on a hill by slipping the clutch. This trick, whereby the clutch is engaged just enough to keep the car from rolling backward, is guaranteed to cost you money. The terrific frictional heat will burn out clutch discs very quickly. If you must stop on a hill for a short interval, keep the clutch depressed and the foot brake on. By setting the hand brake you can reduce the chance of stalling when you attempt to get started. Just ease the hand brake off as you let in the clutch. And if you should stall the engine, you will be in a position to yank on the hand brake before rolling backward.

On certain occasions there is a need to downshift a manual transmission automobile. For example, if a steep hill or slower traffic looms up, second gear may be needed, and the driver should change down from third to second as he approaches the incline or traffic. On other occasions a downshift might be desirable to provide better traction on slippery roads or for engine braking as a hill is descended.

The change to a lower gear can be made in today's cars by merely pushing in the clutch and shoving the lever into a lower gear. This will work but it is not recommended. Like upshifting, downshifting requires that engine speed equal the automobile's speed. Because the whole procedure is reversed, a bit more throttle must be applied when downshifting (conversely, we let up on the throttle when upshifting). We must increase engine speed to equal the speed of the car in the lower gear, because, as you recall, the lower the gear, the faster the engine runs.

Taken in sequence, the change to lower gear is made by depressing the clutch, boosting revs slightly with the throttle, slipping into the next lower gear and then releasing the clutch. (A word of warning should be injected here: with a few exceptions, most manual transmissions have no synchromesh first gear, meaning a great deal of dexterity is required to make a proper downshift into first. Be sure you have digested everything in this chapter and have plenty of experience to boot before you try it.)

Most sports cars carry a tachometer, which indicates engine rpm's and is extremely valuable in telling a driver when to change gears. By reading the tach, he can determine the exact ranges in which his engine provides the most usable power.

A speedometer can be marked with tape or a grease pencil to help the inexperienced driver keep track of his shifting points. The speeds we mentioned earlier can be marked. When the speedometer needle reaches the marked speed, the driver knows it is time for an upshift. These markings would also be helpful in telling the driver when to drop into a lower gear.

Don't expect to "start playing tunes" on your gearbox as soon as you begin driving. Proper gear changing sometimes takes years to learn—and some people never get the hang of it. Just pay attention to what you're doing and, every time you shift gears, ask yourself, "Could I have done it better?" And practice, practice, practice.

6

USING THE BRAKES

Like gear changing, operation of the brakes on a modern automobile appears to be an elementary operation; one merely steps on the pedal and waits for the car to obediently reduce speed. This is essentially the case at slow speeds and on dry, hard-surface pavements. But at higher velocities or under adverse driving conditions use of the brakes requires real deftness and experience.

Before entering into a discussion of braking techniques, it might be worthwhile to note briefly how a braking system on a contemporary automobile works. Basically, it can be explained in two words: Pascal's Law. Blaise Pascal was a seventeenth-century French mathematician and philosopher who formulated the principle that a change of pressure at one point of a confined fluid is communicated undiminished to all parts of the fluid.

In an automobile braking system, the brake lines are filled with just such a "confined fluid." When pressure is applied via the brake pedal from a piston in the master cylinder, pressure is transmitted equally to all four brakes. There the pressure acts on the brake shoes, forcing them against the drums which revolve with the wheels. The friction created by the shoes rubbing against the drums slows the automobile.

Until the middle 1930's most braking systems were mechanically actuated, meaning that the shoes were connected to the brake pedal by cables rather than by hydraulic lines. The cables tended to stretch and brakes of this sort were in need of constant adjustment. The switch to hydraulic brakes, as we call them today, opened the door to more powerful and more reliable stopping.

Until recently it was an unfortunate tradition for domestic automobile manufacturers to ignore the problem of improving braking efficiency. With the adoption of hydraulic systems, many companies used the same basic brakes for several decades despite the fact that their products became heavier and much faster. Several years ago the power brake, which utilizes engine energy via a pump to boost pedal pressure, was adopted amid gales of publicity. Forgotten was the fact that the power unit still acted on the same old brakes that had been in use for twenty years. The results with the power units were impressive at 40 mph, but at 80 mph they were no different from the conventional types in terms of stopping power.

The great enemy of efficient braking is heat. Friction caused by the rubbing of the shoes against the surface of the drums generates terrific heat—the same sort that is built up when you rub the palms of your hands together. This heat causes the surfaces of the brake shoes and drums to lose their abrasive qualities, meaning that the two surfaces tend to slip over each other, reducing the drag which causes the automobile to slow down. This drop in braking efficiency is referred to as "fade."

There is no real way to eliminate the heat unless someone figures out a way to create friction without raising temperatures. What is important to breaking is that the heat created be dissipated properly. Naturally if the heat can be extracted from the drums and shoes before it builds to enormous temperatures we will eliminate brake "fade."

Size in brakes is a factor not only in how much braking area (in terms of shoes and drum surfaces) is available but in how much drum surface can be exposed to the open air—which of course will absorb the heat. To get more braking surface into the airstream, many manufacturers have adopted finned brakes, which expose more drum surface.

Recently our car makers' tendency toward skimpy brakes has been reversed and really effective braking systems are now available on most domestic automobiles. By effective we mean brakes that will slow a car from turnpike speeds or in the descent of a steep hill without fade or pull. With the aluminum finned brake drums that can be purchased as options on a few automobiles, the driver is providing himself with some of the best braking equipment in the world today. It is certainly a far cry from the inadequate systems of even five years ago.

Despite the fact that the brakes have been improved, the driver's responsibility for their proper usage is by no means reduced. Mistakes can be made as easily with the brakes on a post-1960 model car as on a 1940 jalopy.

As an illustration of how important proper braking techniques are, take your automobile out to the nearest hill and let it roll down. Keep the brakes on slightly all the way to the bottom. Then get out and feel one of the wheels. Better wet the end of your finger because the wheel may be as hot as a flat iron. If the hill is long enough and steep enough, you may notice that more pedal pressure is required as you near the bottom. This is brake fade. If permitted to occur in emergency situations (for example, in a high-speed panic stop on a steep downgrade), heat would probably build to a point where the brakes would actually smoke and would increase until there was finally no braking action at all.

Every time you step on the brake pedal think of that heat. Remember that it is causing wear at slow speeds and can cause fade at higher velocities. Now the question remains, how do we prevent or at least reduce heat buildup in our brakes?

The alternate release and application of the brake pedal—generally speaking, two seconds "on" and one second "off"—gives the brakes a cooling-off period every few moments, meaning that temperatures can be kept at proper levels inside the drums. This technique has additional benefits which we will treat in a few moments, but first let's cite a few highway conditions and try to outline the best way to use the brakes in each.

Driving in slow city traffic on dry pavement is probably the environment in which braking technique is the least important. Of course efficient stopping power is crucial, but at 30–35 mph fade is not the factor that it is on the open road. For this reason, on-off operation of the brakes in the city is not essential. Normally one smooth application of the brakes to slow you from 30 mph for a red light will do no damage and cause no fade. Obviously the stop should be made gently, with the car rolling quietly to a halt. Charging up to the light and then slamming on the brakes is abusive to the car and seldom gains time.

City driving becomes more hazardous when the pavement is wet. Then the friction between the tires and the pavement is reduced, meaning the brakes may stop the wheels from rotating but the automobile will continue on, literally skating on the slippery surface. We refer to this as "locking up the brakes" and state firmly it is never recommended under any driving situation. When you find the surface slippery in city driving, *then* use the on-off technique. (Notice we do not use the phrase "pump the brakes." Pumping implies rapid depression and release of the brake pedal, which is not advised.) Apply the brakes until the wheels almost stop turning. Then release the brakes, then reapply. By continuing this action you will find speed falls off very quickly no matter how slippery the pavement. One word of warning: when using the brakes on icy or wet surfaces, don't slam the pedal down, especially if you have power brakes. A hard application, even for a second, where the tires have no grip, can lock things up. Depress the pedal smoothly and firmly at all times.

In driving on the open road or turnpike, brake usage falls into three general categories: light braking for corners, a slower car, etc.; braking for stops at intersections, railroad crossings, etc.; and emergency braking where reducing speed in the shortest possible distance is crucial.

In dry weather, light braking can normally be made with a couple of applications of the pedal. Fade is no real factor here and flawless technique is not important. Only one word of advice is necessary: as you approach a corner, a hill or other situation where you know light braking will be required, *leave yourself a margin* in the event the brakes fail. For example, if a bend in the highway is coming up, back off on the throttle early enough so that it can be negotiated without brakes. Then, if the brakes have failed—and make no mistake, they do fail on occasion—you will not find yourself in a hopeless situation. You may motor through the corner a bit faster than you intended, but at least you'll get through. This margin is not just for sissies or little old ladies. Most race drivers leave a margin for safety, choosing their braking point for a corner so that it can be negotiated if the brakes unexpectedly disappear. One final note on braking for corners: get your braking over *before* you enter the corner. Braking interferes with steering control and can be dangerous in corners, especially on slippery pavement.

Naturally in situations requiring full stops from highway speeds it would be ridiculous to recommend leaving enough margin so the car would coast to a halt without brakes. However, some margin can be provided, meaning that braking for an intersection, etc., should be started early enough so that the car will be under control at a *reduced speed* when the stopping point is reached. This at least gives the driver some chance to take emergency evasive action at a relatively safe speed. Obviously coming up to a stop sign full bore and then slamming on the brakes leaves one in a poor position to do much of anything besides duck.

This "margin" that we speak of cannot be translated in terms of feet and mph and given to you in a neat little formula. It is something that you as a driver will have to feel. As a beginner, your judgment will be poor, but as you gain a sense of what your automobile is capable of under certain conditions, that margin will become more apparent.

As we said in the previous chapter, engine braking through the use of the gearbox can be valuable in reducing speed. If the driver suddenly finds himself without brakes, one of the first corrective measures to be taken is to shift to a lower gear for more engine braking (more on this in Chapter 12). Downshifting for better stopping power is also recommended for mountain driving or on slippery pavements. However, unless a loss-of-brakes situation arises, the downshift should be made *before* the hill or the slippery pavement, etc., is reached. Unless a driver has extensive experience with downshifting techniques (in the case of standard transmissions) he should concentrate on conventional driving. Fumbling with a downshift in the middle of a hill can only divert an inexperienced driver's attention and may spell disaster.

It should be noted here that the "parking" or "emergency" brake is not used in normal highway driving. It is valuable in holding the car in place when stopped and has limited usage in emergency stopping situations (see Chapter 12).

Coming to a full stop from higher open-road speeds requires the same on-off braking system used elsewhere. A firm application of the brakes to begin the slowing process, then release for a second or so, then back on the brake pedal is recommended. Remember that the higher the speed, the more pedal pressure is required. At over 70 mph you will probably have to give the brakes a couple of good healthy punches before any discernible braking action begins.

An emergency stop from high turnpike speeds can present two major problems. One, the driver can keep the brakes on so long and so hard that he will literally fade them out of action, and two, he may clamp them on so tightly that the brakes will lock up. At best this latter situation will send the car skidding along the highway. At the worst it will throw the automobile completely out of control.

When making a panic stop from over 50 mph, give the pedal a hard application. Hold it on for maybe two or three seconds, then back off to cool the drums and shoes. Fade can be identified through a sponginess in the brake pedal and it normally requires more foot pressure. Just be ready for it when it happens. Normally, on level highways, the car can be stopped before fade eliminates braking action entirely.

The really dangerous part of an emergency braking action comes when the drums and wheels are locked up. This of course means that the tires are no longer turning and one segment of rubber is skating along the pavement. Frictional heat will build quickly to a point where the rubber melts, reducing adhesion even more (and accounting for those ugly black marks on the road). Theoretically, the farther the tire slides, the hotter it gets, progressively reducing adhesion.

In an emergency, brake hard up to the point of locking the brakes, then release them. When you hear the

71

screech of rubber and feel the automobile sliding along the pavement, *get off the brakes* for a split second. With some sort of obstacle looming up, the natural reaction is to stand on the brakes as hard as you can and stay there until the automobile stops. To brake properly in a situation like this you must overcome that tendency. If you don't, the chances are one in ten you won't stop in time.

Locked-up brakes can also cause vicious skids. When stopping, a heavy percentage of the automobile's weight transfers to the front wheels. If one of the front brakes locks up while the other still rotates, the automobile may pivot on the stopped wheel and skid off the highway. As we said in Chapter 3, you may not realize that you have a brake that tends to lock until you encounter an emergency stopping situation. Consequently, be ready for it when it occurs. If the automobile begins to slew off line under heavy braking, correct the wheel in the direction of the skid and get off the brakes for a second. Continue the on-off sequence, making corrective steering movements at the same time.

Naturally the same techniques apply to braking on the open road in adverse weather conditions. However, because the brakes will have an exaggerated tendency to lock up on slippery pavement, the margin for slowing must be extended. Rather than beginning to slow for an intersection at X yards, the distance should probably be doubled. Under extremely slip-

Icy, snow-covered roads demand that the braking point be moved well back. Though the curve pictured is still at a considerable distance, now is the time for the driver to be absolutely sure that his car is under control for its negotiation.

pery conditions, a driver should remain in a lower gear or range to provide added braking power.

It would be a good idea to try some braking on a wet or ice-covered deserted parking lot or open area. This will give you some idea of what to expect and will accentuate the concept of doubling your margin. Make no mistake about it, there is no more night-marish sensation in driving than to apply the brakes on slippery pavement and find the automobile has begun a long, heart-stopping slide.

Don't forget that moisture, either rain, snow or heavy fog, can interfere with braking action. Normally dampness on the shoes and drums will cause the brakes to grab, sometimes locking the wheels. When it is wet, apply the brakes gently before you begin serious braking. The friction built up in this initial light engagement will wipe the braking surfaces free of moisture and will permit you to stop normally. But, like so many other facets of smart driving, this little brake-drying precaution cannot be taken unless you give yourself that margin of safety. It boils down to this, if you try to use your brakes in adverse weather conditions as you would normally, you will have troubles, and that's all there is to it.

In hilly or mountainous country the force of gravity joins with the kinetic energy of the automobile to make stopping even more difficult. It doesn't take a degree in physics to determine that a 3,500-pound car running 50 mph down the side of a hill is considerably harder to stop than it would be running at the same speed on the level.

Because of the heavier burden placed on the brakes in stopping downhill, a real deftness on the pedal is necessary. Overuse of the brakes in the mountains can leave the linings smoldering and the drums red hot within seconds.

Imagine a driver as he rolls down a long, relatively straight hillside. Running at a steady 50 mph, he applies the brakes lightly at the top and keeps them on, unwittingly permitting heat in the drums to build to awesome levels. Suddenly, as he nears the bottom, the road twists into a tight curve, negotiable at only 25 mph. He clamps on the brakes harder, attempting to cut his speed in half. Nothing happens. He frantically rams the brake pedal to the floor. Still no response. Our hero literally "fades" out of the picture.

His mistake was in letting his brake temperatures rise by never releasing the pedal on the way down. Although such a stunt may not end in a crash, the wear on shoes and drums is terrific under such conditions. Lesson: use your brakes with great care while descending a steep hill.

If you find as you are traveling down a hillside that the automobile surges ahead every time you release the brakes for cooling, chances are you are running in too high a gear. If your transmission is automatic, drop into a lower range. If you feel experienced enough with a standard shift, also change down. However, be sure not to "miss a shift" in a situation like this. If a lower gear cannot be engaged, you might find it difficult to get back into the original gear. This of course means you would make the trip to the bottom without any engine braking at all—and probably at terrifying speed.

The wise thing is to determine whether or not a lower gear is needed at the top of the hill and change down there. Look over the terrain and the condition of the road and check the warning signs, if any, at the top. These will give you a fair idea of what lies ahead. If you are in doubt, use a lower gear.

The real key to braking in the mountains lies at the crest of the hills. Here, as we just said, you must make complete preparations for the descent. By habit, a check of the brakes should be made whenever a steep hill is encountered. A touch of the pedal to be sure hydraulic pressure is up is all that is necessary.

If you are a resident of a mountainous area or plan to do a great deal of driving in the mountains, be sure that your brakes get a maximum amount of cooling. Toward this objective, fender skirts for the rear wheels or non-stock full wheel discs are not advised. Both types of ornaments restrict air flow around the brake drums and can add to the danger of fade and rapid wear of brake linings.

Though few people realize it, an automobile's stopping (and going) power is greatly affected by the amount of weight it carries. If an automobile is carrying one person and no luggage, it will stop considerably faster than if its load includes four people and plenty of baggage. Figuring each person's weight at 150 pounds and a like amount for the suitcases, etc., a driver can add 600 pounds to his automobile without realizing it. This weight will cut stopping efficiency, especially in the mountains. Use extra caution if your automobile is heavily loaded.

Slippery road surfaces are the major hazard to proper braking in the mountains. Because of the added pull of gravity, a locked front wheel on ice can cause a car to swap ends before the driver has a chance to correct. The same situation on level ground might cause the automobile to "wag its tail" one way or the other without any dangerous aftereffects. But on a steep incline the automobile has a much greater tendency to spin as soon as its rear end gets out of line. Therefore, keeping the brakes from locking up on slippery surfaces in the mountains becomes a matter of life and death.

Use a lower gear on the way down a hill if the road surface is uniformly icy or wet. If the pavement is patched with ice or packed snow, be sure your braking is completed *before* you hit the patches. Brake hard if you have to right up to the edge of the ice, then let off. This will permit you to cross the slick spot with all wheels turning.

Be prepared for anything in the mountains. For example, the weather may be fine down in the valleys, warm and dry. But at higher altitudes a quick shower may have caused a little rivulet to flow across the highway. When darkness comes the temperature drops below freezing and there it is—a treacherous little patch of ice on an otherwise dry pavement.

In summation, poor-weather braking in the mountains requires that two rules be remembered: (1) always brake on dry surfaces and in straight lines if possible, and (2) *never* let your speed increase to a point where emergency braking measures may be necessary.

There is no fast way down a slippery mountainside. And in the final analysis, restraint and good judgment will pay off for you under these circumstances more than all the driving skill in the world.

7

CORNERING

Treating each phase of driving as an isolated operation, the one which probably requires the most skill and judgment is that of negotiating a corner at highway speeds. In a straight line, the modern automobile is a pleasant, docile beast with excellent manners. However, passage through a corner calls into play forces of nature that may give that same good-natured vehicle a rather waspish disposition. Handled correctly, there is nothing about cornering that should stimulate any fear or upset in a driver, but mistakes can be made unless a clear idea exists of what energies are developed in such an operation and what can be done to control them.

Engineers have spent decades attempting to make automobiles safer and easier to handle while turning, yet a heavy percentage of one-car accidents are still caused by drivers losing control on curves. Mishaps of this sort are unnecessary because any curve can be negotiated if a little forethought and common sense are used.

Isaac Newton would maintain, if he were living, that an automobile doesn't want to go around a curve. His first law of motion says a body continues in uniform motion in a straight line unless acted upon by a force. You can probably remember, while riding in an automobile, being forced against the door when the driver made a sharp left-hand turn. This is Newton's law in action. Your body was trying to continue in a straight line. And so was the car. Only the friction between the tires and the road surface prevented it from continuing in that direction.

You have seen the trick of a bucket of water being spun so quickly over a person's head that the water remained inside without a drop being spilled. You may also have seen carnival daredevils riding motorcycles around the sheer walls of a cylindrical chamber. both of these tricks utilize what is called centrifugal force.

Take a small object and tie a string around it. Then spin it rapidly around your head. You can feel centrifugal force pulling the object away from you. If you let go of the string the object will rocket away. The same force is acting upon an automobile when it negotiates a curve. Let the centrifugal force become too great, which would happen with excessive speed, and the automobile will react just like the object when you release the string.

Cars vary in their reaction to centrifugal force, depending on the suspension layout, the overall weight, the center of gravity, etc. Some try to go straight ahead when the wheel is turned. Others turn readily enough, only to have their rear ends pivot outward.

Ideally, an automobile should point exactly where the steering wheel is turned. It should take no more effort or movement of the steering wheel to turn a car at either high or low speeds. Some automobiles have this quality, called neutral steer.

Most American cars understeer. This means the automobile is reluctant to point itself into a corner, forcing the driver to turn more and more as he rounds the bend.

Other automobiles oversteer or, as we said before, the rear end tries to swing outward. With an oversteering car, the driver must constantly reduce the amount of steering lock he is using as he motors through a bend. Why? Because the automobile is actually trying to spin, forcing the driver to make the same basic corrections that he would if the tail had skidded around on ice.

On a constant-radius bend the driver of a neutral-steering car would only have to turn the wheel once at the entrance and it would travel around as if on rails. The driver of an understeering car would have to keep turning more and more as he rounded the bend, and the driver of the oversteerer would have to reduce steering lock.

Most passenger automobiles steer neutrally at low speeds. It is only at higher speeds, when the physical forces begin to get stronger, that oversteer and understeer become apparent. An automobile might be perfectly obedient at 45 mph. But at 60 mph it might

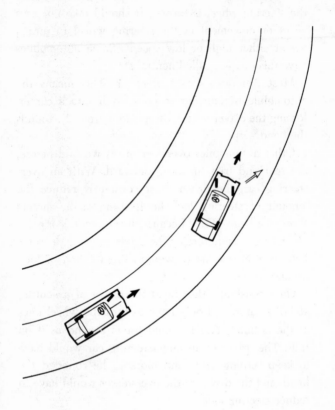

In an understeering car the automobile continues to angle in a straight line and the driver is forced to turn his wheels progressively more to the left as he passes through the bend. Note that with understeer the front wheels begin to slide first.

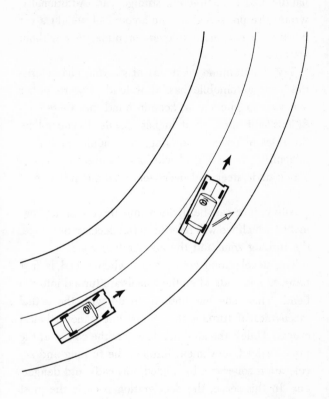

In an oversteering car the tendency is for the rear wheels to slide first. Here the driver has been forced to reduce the amount his wheels are turned as he rounds the corner (much as he would if he began to slide slightly on a patch of ice).

handle like a completely strange car. Additionally, wrong tire pressures and the amount of weight a car is carrying can increase over- or understeer without warning.

Try to determine what sort of steering characteristics your automobile has. If it tends toward either oversteer or understeer, keep in mind that these conditions will intensify at higher speeds. If you follow the rules of proper cornering, you should have little difficulty. (We will deal with how to overcome emergency understeer and oversteer situations in Chapter 12.)

Any corner can be divided into three distinct segments, which we will refer to as the deceleration zone, the turning zone and the acceleration zone.

The deceleration zone begins when speed is first reduced and ends when the wheels are turned into the bend. This zone has nothing to do with the actual mechanics of turning the corner but is nevertheless crucial. Unless the automobile enters the corner at the proper speed, movement through the turning and acceleration zones can be ragged, unsteady and dangerous. In this sense, the deceleration zone is the most important of the three, because poor judgment or improper action here will be compounded in the remaining zones.

For a gentle bend in a wide highway, the deceleration zone may involve merely an easing up on the throttle or a light application of the brakes. By way of contrast, a tight downhill corner may require heavy braking if entry is to be made properly.

The important thing to remember about the deceleration zone is that it ends when the front wheels begin to turn. *All slowing for a corner should be completed while the car is traveling in a straight line.* A driver is asking for trouble if he tries to slow down his automobile in the turning zone.

The size of the deceleration zone is determined by the tightness of the corner and the speed at which it is being approached. It is a matter of judgment as to when the zone is entered but always give yourself enough margin so that a safe speed has been reached well before the turning zone.

From the deceleration zone the driver makes a smooth transition to the turning zone. This is the area from the point the wheels are turned to the "center" of the corner. If you imagine a curve as a circle and the path of the automobile as a straight line running tangent to the circle, the picture will become clearer. All curves, be they on a geometry teacher's blackboard or on the open road, have a center.

In addition to moving the steering wheel, the driver has an important function to carry out with the throttle. Power should be used in both the turning and acceleration zones. An automobile is much safer and easier to handle with power on. Throttle application in the turning zone should be light and constant or what is sometimes referred to as "feathered."

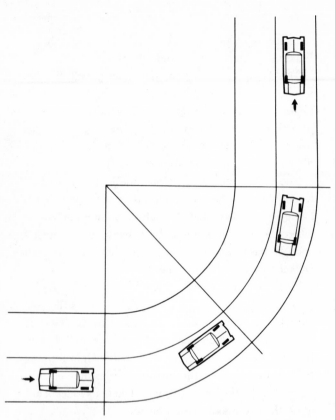

The three segments of a corner. The car at the bottom left is in the deceleration zone, where all braking should be completed. The second vehicle from the bottom is in the turning zone, where steady speed is maintained. Note that this vehicle is very near the apex or center of the corner. This line is the demarcation between the turning and acceleration zones. The third car from the bottom is in the process of exiting the corner and is accelerating back to normal cruising speed. The automobile at the top right is on its way at the legal limit, having successfully negotiated the bend.

The acceleration zone begins immediately after the center or tangent has been passed. From here on the automobile is exiting the corner and a gradual buildup of speed is possible.

With the concepts of the three segments of a corner and the proper line firmly in mind, let's run through a typical curve on the open road.

The initial operation in the negotiation of a curve is mental. This occurs well down the road, before any change in speed or direction is begun. The driver assays the condition ahead, taking note of the approximate radius of the curve, the extent of visibility, the width of the highway, the condition of its surface and oncoming traffic.

The entry into the deceleration zone is begun by lifting the throttle and beginning the braking procedure (if necessary). It should be noted here that all movements on the throttle must be executed smoothly. When we speak of backing off on the throttle or applying power, we don't mean abrupt on-off movements. Try to make transitions between acceleration and deceleration as gently as possible.

As the end of the deceleration zone is reached, the speed should be reduced to the necessary level and the automobile should be positioned near the center of its lane. About the time the wheel is turned into the corner, begin to apply a slight amount of power, just enough to keep the car's speed steady. At the halfway

87

point of the bend, or the tangent, begin a gradual increase of speed, again concentrating on smoothness.

Errors made early will compound themselves as you proceed through a corner. Not enough braking in the deceleration zone will mean you traverse the turning zone too rapidly, which will in turn swing you too wide as you exit. This occurs because maximum centrifugal force comes to bear shortly after the tangent has been passed, forcing the car to the outside.

Be more wary in negotiating right-hand bends than left handers. This is recommended because an error in a right-hand corner will force the automobile into the oncoming lane of traffic, making a head-on collision possible. Conversely, trouble while turning left will send the car onto the shoulder of the road. This is especially important in poor weather when the possibility of skidding is strongest.

In addition to reducing the chances of spinning off the road, a slow, smooth entry into a corner places you in a better position to avoid trouble from other cars. If an automobile in the other lane goes out of control, you will be able to take evasive action if you aren't on the "ragged edge of control."

Though we will deal with correcting slides in detail in Chapter 12, let it be said for now that a minor slide or skid in a corner does not necessarily mean disaster. If the tail of the automobile begins to slide on a slippery spot, merely turn the wheel in the same direction until it gets back in line. And by using the hand posi-

In the deceleration zone. The right hand has been dropped to the four-o'clock position on the wheel in preparation for entering the corner. All braking should be about completed and the driver should be prepared to make a smooth entrance into the bend.

In the turning zone steady, light throttle application is essential. Note that the automobile is positioned near the inside of the turn, allowing it to travel through an arc of near-maximum width. Speed should be reduced to a point where only minor steering corrections are necessary once the proper line has been determined.

The acceleration zone calls for a gentle increase in power and the reduction of steering lock to return the automobile to straight-line travel. Mistakes made in the deceleration or turning zones may manifest themselves at this point, so be absolutely sure the car is under control before returning to your normal cruising speed.

Recommended hand positions
for making a tight right turn.
Top left to right, deceleration
zone, turning zone; bottom,
acceleration zone.

90

Excellent example of a negative camber corner.

tions recommended in Chapter 2, you will be able to turn the wheel easily in the widest possible arc in either direction should a slide occur.

You probably have noticed that the turns on most race tracks are banked, meaning the outer perimeter is considerably higher than the inner. This is done to reduce centrifugal force, permitting the race cars to run faster. Today many highway turns are banked in a similar fashion, enabling passenger automobiles to negotiate them more safely. If you notice an approaching bend is banked, don't change your technique. Drive through as you would normally.

Topographical conditions may be such that a curve will slant to the outside or have what is called "negative camber." Be extra cautious on curves of this type.

91

Instead of helping to keep the automobile on the highway, the negative banking will offer no resistance at all, making it relatively easy to slide.

Each corner varies in length, radius, banking, surface, etc., and must be taken differently. Even at the Indianapolis Motor Speedway, where the four corners are identical, drivers negotiate each in a slightly different way.

Treat each bend in the road with respect. If you enter a corner with prudence, the odds are in your favor that you will negotiate it in safety. Underestimate the challenge of cornering and you may be headed for trouble.

8

DRIVING IN URBAN TRAFFIC

If you've never ridden with a cab driver through mid-Manhattan rush-hour traffic, you have missed one of the most hair-raising passenger car trips this side of the Daytona 500. Sitting helpless in the back seat, you watch in amazement as the cabbie slashes through the clogged streets, now on the brakes, now on the throttle, his horn blaring incessantly. Somehow you make it to your destination and you climb out, dazed and thankful. As you pay the driver, you cannot help but notice the dented sides of his automobile, evidence that other trips have not been so successful.

New York cab drivers are probably the best heavy-traffic motorists in the world. Day in and day out they cut and shoot through the United States' busiest streets with amazingly few serious accidents. But they pay the price. To make time, they use their machines to the limit, placing an enormous strain on clutches, brakes and differentials. This, in addition to minor scrapes that disfigure the entire body within a short period, makes cab duty extremely difficult on an automobile. Despite one or two major overhauls, the average cab is an irreparable shambles in two years.

Unless you are willing to risk abuse of your automobile, arrests and even collisions, there is no foolproof way to go fast in traffic. Even driving as desperately as you can, cutting in and out of lanes, passing on the right, leaping away from stoplights, etc., provides no guarantee that you will get where you are going any sooner. A case in point: In 1948, famous Indianapolis race driver Cliff Bergere made a nationwide tour in behalf of safe driving. In each of the four hundred cities he visited, Cliff made two runs over a predetermined course through the city's heaviest traffic. On the initial trip he broke every rule of sensible driving, then drove as safely as possible the second time around. On trips averaging 2–4 miles, Cliff was never more than *60 seconds* slower on the second journey, while driving carefully, than on the first, when he performed like a maniac!

On today's urban highways, both dual and single lane, 30 mph is about the absolute maximum speed that can be legally averaged. This means running a steady 40–45 mph on the freeway sections and about 30 mph in the more congested areas. Averaging 40 mph would be a highly dangerous undertaking. To maintain such a speed the driver would have to take advantage of every opening in traffic and consistently exceed the legal limit. On a run of five miles, the driver who averaged 40 mph would arrive at his destination a mere 2.5 minutes before the person who averaged 30 mph! How much is that interval worth? Certainly not the risks involved.

City traffic can be a nightmare. Automobiles come at you from all sides, pedestrians wander everywhere, movement is interrupted by constant stops for lights, for turning vehicles, for traffic jams, etc. One day a section of street will be clear, making travel a breeze. Twenty-four hours later it can be plugged tight with a honking mass of automobiles. An accident or an excavation may back up traffic for miles. On many thoroughfares three or four lines of traffic may be forced to funnel into one lane for a narrow bridge or a toll booth. Is this any environment in which to make time?

The first rule of traffic driving is relax and take it easy. Reconcile yourself to doing that and allow enough time to reach your destination without overextending yourself or your automobile.

If you find yourself short of time, the attempt to rush will immediately affect your composure. Your temper will get shorter and you will try all the harder, causing the odds for an accident to leapfrog.

It has been proved that the best (and safest) time in traffic can be made by maintaining the same general speed as most of the other automobiles. If you try to run faster, you are being forced into continuous passing situations, and with cars turning and lane hopping in front of you the danger is obvious. Driving slower than the flow of traffic is also both unsafe and rude. You may think you are being extra cautious, but in reality you are setting the stage for an accident. The

Relax in city traffic. Keep to the right unless making a left turn and try to maintain a steady speed in keeping with traffic conditions.

drivers behind are forced to pass, thereby increasing their risks and adding to the overall congestion.

It is important in city traffic to keep track of what is going on not only in front but in back and on both sides. Heavy traffic is in constant flux and a dangerous situation can form in seconds. Keep your eyes and head moving. Check the rear-view mirror every few moments and before every speed and directional change. Try to keep a mental file of the location and movements of the vehicles behind. Glance from side to side periodically to be sure no one is overtaking.

Don't focus your attention on the automobiles nearest you. If visibility permits, watch two or three cars ahead and behind. Should an emergency situation develop, chances are these automobiles will be involved.

What if you were running along a crowded street, third in a line of six automobiles, and the first one made a sudden stop? You should have been observing what was going on in order to take evasive action. But what about the cars behind? Maybe the sixth one in line is running much too fast to stop. Under these circumstances, that automobile's actions will have as much bearing on you as those of the lead car.

A rule of safe driving states that one car-length interval should be kept between you and the car ahead for every 10 mph of speed. At 50 mph you should maintain a five-car-length space between your front bumper and the car ahead. In some states this has been written into the traffic lawbooks.

The first time you try to abide by this rule on a freeway or a crowded street you will probably find someone squeezing into the space you leave. At 30 mph, that three-car space will generally be too much temptation for someone behind and he will hop into it.

Our only recommendation is that you back off a little bit to open the right interval between yourself and the driver who has just cut in. Give *yourself* a break. Driving is not a competition where you lose points every time someone passes you. As long as you maintain a steady speed and the proper interval and stay out of other people's way, you are doing your most competent and courteous driving. If another driver does something stupid, give him all the room you can. The way he's acting, you may need it to keep out of his way.

It's strange, but courtesy and common sense parallel each other. In most cases, the smartest piece of driving is the most courteous. Yet it's impossible for us to say piously, "At all times be full of courtesy and good will toward your fellow drivers." As human beings, we are all subject to fits of rage and impatience and any such recommendation would be unrealistic and hypocritical. However, we can say, "Be courteous, if not for the other fellow, at least for your own sake." If you cannot develop any courtesy even in the cause of self-preservation, you belong on a psychiatrist's couch, not behind the wheel of an automobile.

Because of the proximity of other cars, proper signaling is crucial in city traffic. Where a blinking turn signal can be seen for hundreds of feet on the open road, it may be obscured by other automobiles on urban streets. Hand signals should supplement the turn indicators wherever possible. This is especially important when making left-hand turns, where danger exists from both oncoming and overtaking traffic. Obviously, common sense should be your guide. If you are making a turn on a slippery, nearly deserted street, you will want both hands on the wheel rather than one waving out the window at nonexistent traffic. But in any situation where another driver might not understand your movements, use *both* hand and light signals.

Hand signal for a left turn.

Hand signal for a right turn.

Stop signal.

In line with our policy of restraint in city driving, passing and lane hopping should be kept to a minimum. When congestion is encountered, choose a lane and try to stay in it. In two-lane traffic, the right lane is preferable for through traffic and right turns while the left should be used for turns in that direction and for passing. On a three-lane urban thoroughfare stay in the middle file unless you want to turn, then use one of the other two lanes.

Don't keep trying to pass cars. You won't get a nickel in prize money or a peep of applause if you beat the next guy downtown. Nobody much cares whether you pass him, and is the effort worth all the strain on your nerves and your automobile? Relax in traffic. Most passing done here saves about as much time as running to the front of a train to get to the next station faster.

Of course some passing and movement from lane to lane are necessary. Automobiles turning or running at slow speeds may require passing. Before you turn out, twist your head and *take a look*. Do not rely on your rear-view mirror. The blind spot may be large enough to hide a moving van. And be sure that you check visually *before* you turn out or accelerate. Looking after you have begun to change lanes only makes your automobile more difficult to bring under control should the way be blocked.

Though found primarily in villages, diagonal parking is still common. Because the view of the driver backing out of a parking space is obstructed, keep a sharp lookout. Diagonally parked cars also provide plenty of hiding places for jaywalking pedestrians and playing children.

The potentially dangerous driving situations in urban traffic are infinite in number. Thousands of accidents occur each year at intersections, many involving two automobiles as they meet at right angles.

The chain-reaction crash, wherein several cars ram each other like a row of dominoes, is also common.

If you are crossing an intersection and suddenly spot another vehicle rushing at you from either side, turn your wheels *away* from the direction in which it is approaching. This will cause the collision to be more of a glancing blow than a direct hit. If the car is coming at you from the right, be sure not to turn left into the path of approaching traffic. You may be trading a minor dent in the side for a head-on collision.

More grills and trunks are smashed in chain-reaction accidents than in any other type of mishap. Most begin when the lead car stops suddenly and one of the automobiles following is traveling too fast to stop in time and mashes the whole line together. If you are observing proper space intervals, and use proper braking techniques, a quick stop by the automobile ahead should not provide any emergency. But, if this situation arises, check your rear-view mirror as you stop. Someone behind may not be able to slow in time, meaning that you are about to receive a hard slam in the rear end. In this case, try to snug in as close as possible to the car ahead. Then, when you are hit, the impact will ram you into the vehicle in front but the force will be absorbed by the weight of two cars rather than one. This action may mean the loss of your grillwork as well as the trunk lid, but it will significantly reduce the chance of personal injury. If the accident cannot be prevented, be sure that your wheels are pointed straight ahead at the moment of impact. This will prevent your automobile from being bounced into another lane, where you might be hit by another car traveling at a much higher speed.

While waiting for oncoming traffic to pass before making a left-hand turn, also be sure your wheels are straight ahead. Then, should you be hit from behind, your car will not roll into the path of the approaching automobiles.

Never let your horn be a substitute for controlling your car. Use the horn as a warning device *while* you bring your automobile under complete control. Too many drivers merely honk their horns as they approach a potentially dangerous situation without slowing or preparing themselves to take evasive measures. If the warning from their horn is ignored and the situation materializes, they find themselves completely unready. Use your horn as a supplement, not a substitute, for safe driving.

Don't make the mistake of believing that seat belts are only valuable on the open road. Though speeds are generally higher and the collision forces greater on rural highways, many people receive grievous injuries in accidents that occur at relatively slow velocities. In a collision at even a modest 30 mph, the doors stand a good chance of flying open, sending the passengers sprawling on the pavement. Install seat belts and use them even if you are traveling no farther than the supermarket.

We wish that we could provide you with a series of pat rules that would assure you of safe, easy city driving. Unfortunately this is impossible. The only substitutes we can suggest are restraint, attentiveness and courtesy. By taking your time, controlling your temper, keeping your eyes open and giving yourself and the other fellow a break, you will be putting forth your best effort under the city's demanding driving conditions.

9

ON THE OPEN ROAD

Open-road motoring, with its high speeds and constantly changing topography, is the most challenging environment for the driver. All the skills of handling an automobile are called upon and proper technique is more important here than anywhere else.

Highway driving combines the hazards of urban driving with cruising speeds nearly equal to those of turnpikes and freeways. (By way of definition, we refer to normal roads with two-way traffic as "highways." "Turnpikes," "thruways," "freeways" are limited-access roadways with directional traffic separated by a grass strip, guardrail, curb, or other divider. The resultant conditions demand the very best from the driver and his automobile.

Every mile of open road is different, from the ribbons of pavement that stretch across the Western plains to the narrow roadways that twist their way round the Appalachian Mountains of the East.

Speeds of 70 mph and over can be safely and legally maintained on thousands of miles of roads in the United States. And equal mileage exists where half that speed is the absolute limit.

Variations like this call for versatility on the part of

Drive through rural crossroads as you would on city streets. Often without warning you may come upon sleepy little junctions like the one pictured here. Exercise real caution in localities such as this, and watch especially for children playing, running dogs, and slow-moving traffic.

the driver. He must be able to adapt himself to every sort of highway condition, and this is not so easy as it sounds. For example, many city dwellers are poor road drivers. They are so specialized in the art of urban driving that many find it difficult to meet the different demands of the open road. In fact, shortly after the New York Thruway opened, it was discovered that a heavy percentage of the accidents involved residents of metropolitan New York. It appeared that many of them had become so used to maneuvering in close quarters at a maximum of 45 mph that the open road at 60 mph was like driving on Mars. Moving at higher rates of speed presented new problems to these drivers, who were handicapped by limited versatility.

Finding a *comfortable* speed should be the first duty of the driver when he begins a highway trip. This is the speed at which the driver and automobile seem to function best. It may vary from day to day, depending on the weather, the road, the driver's capabilities and the automobile's mechanical condition. This speed should fall somewhere near the legal limit. If you don't feel like going this fast, be sure to stay in the lane farthest to the right.

Stay within the speed limit! The mental strain and distraction on the driver who is traveling above the legal speed can greatly increase the danger of an accident. A driver barreling along faster than he legally should be is on the lookout for the police, and his concentration on the road is considerably reduced. The sight of a suspicious automobile in the rear-view mirror will force him to slow down until it can be identified. An erratic pace, punctuated by bursts of great speed and periods of cautious creeping, generally results. And, with unmarked police cars roaming the roads plus more and more radar checks, the odds are the speedster will be caught anyway.

Much of the danger in highway driving would be eliminated if you never overtook any vehicles. This would nullify the need for passing, a tactic which demands plenty of practice before it can be executed properly.

A driver is in his most vulnerable position when passing another automobile on a two-way two-lane highway. He is running in the wrong lane, straight at oncoming traffic. He would have trouble avoiding the vehicle he is passing, should its driver make an unexpected turn or swerve. And his chances would be slim should a vehicle turn into the left lane.

A passing position should not be entered impulsively. The roadway should be absolutely clear before you pull out. Be sure you are fully aware of the situation ahead, and if things look doubtful, wait. Again, no prizes are on the line if you make it, but the penalty is stiff for a near miss.

There are no situations in which you *must* pass. If the road is unclear or oncoming traffic is heavy, you can wait even if the vehicle you are following is slogging along at 5 mph. Be patient; your chance to get by will come soon enough.

It is best to pass a car only when the lane for oncoming traffic is completely clear. However, on long straight stretches passes can be executed in complete safety even though other cars are approaching in the distance. But, before trying this, you must have a good idea of how much time is needed to pass the car ahead. While passing, keep a rough count of the number of seconds it takes to get around vehicles. By observing the average amount of time it takes approaching cars to reach you and comparing those figures with your passing time, you can gain a fair idea of when passing is safe. But never count on being able to determine the speed of oncoming vehicles. This is nearly impossible, even for the most experienced drivers. Passing ability is something that should develop with experience, so don't overdo it until you have a few years of open-road driving under your belt. The best advice here is to be patient and never pass unless you are *sure* you can do so in complete safety.

After you have decided the road is clear to pass and have made sure that no one is passing or is about to pass you, make a habit of snapping on the left turn signal before pulling out. This blinking light will not only warn drivers behind but may be spotted by approaching motorists. On occasion a passing car will be mistaken for an automobile traveling in the opposite direction. Chances of this error will be reduced if the driver up ahead sees your signal.

At night a flash of your headlights on high beam will warn the driver ahead of your intention to pass. In daylight, if you have any fear that he may not be aware of your desire, give the horn a light, courteous tap before pulling by.

Once you get into the left lane don't dally. Accelerate briskly to get by the vehicle ahead. However, don't accelerate so quickly that you wouldn't be able to slow down and duck back into line if some unseen danger suddenly appeared. If you are forced to use full throttle to get around an automobile before oncoming traffic arrives, you have made a poorly judged pass.

Make a mental note of this and try not to let it happen again.

You should continue in the opposite lane until you catch sight of the car you just passed in the rear-view mirror. This provides an ample lead to pull in ahead without cutting him off. Before turning back into line, flick on the right-hand turn signal to insure that you have made your intentions absolutely clear. *Don't* forget to turn the signals off when you have returned to the right-hand lane. Nothing is a surer indication that a driver isn't paying attention to his driving than a turn indicator that keeps blinking miles after his last turn. And nothing can be more confusing to other drivers.

If you have more than a normal load of luggage or passengers on board, remember that your acceleration will be reduced. Allow lengthier passing margins than normal, especially when towing a trailer. Car performance will not only be cut but more space will be needed to fit into line.

When a driver is thoughtless enough to meander along a main thoroughfare at 30 mph, faster traffic soon backs up behind him. It is not uncommon to come upon five to ten automobiles trailing behind a slowpoke of this sort, all awaiting an opportunity to pass. The temptation is to pass the whole string in one grand gesture. The best solution is to let the cars ahead work their way around before you try to pass. Of course you will upon occasion come upon two or three cars

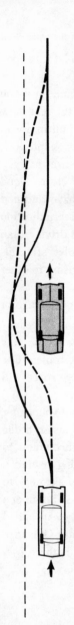

The solid line in the diagram indicates the proper way to pass; the dotted line shows the most dangerous way. In the approved way the car in the rear is pulled into the passing lane well behind the vehicle that is being overtaken. This technique has two advantages: (1) It permits the driver to take a good look at conditions ahead before increasing speed. If the pass looks unsafe, he can easily pull back into line. The improper way places the passing car beside the one being overtaken before conditions ahead can be determined. (2) The passing vehicle is able to attain passing speed *before* the car ahead is reached. This allows the driver to return to his own lane in the shortest possible time. The incorrect technique forces the driver to accelerate while he is still beside the car he is passing, and this slows down the entire process.

Give the driver who is passing plenty of room. Here a car is approaching in the opposite lane, making it necessary for the driver of the white automobile to hurry a bit to get back into line. It is your obligation to slow down to give the white car a chance to return to the right-hand lane more quickly. The danger of a head-on collision between the passing and the approaching cars has not been entirely eliminated, and you want to be sure that you have enough distance for evasive moves should any accident occur.

all running slowly. Be sure, if you try a multi-car pass, that you use your horn or lights to warn the other drivers. And *never* try this maneuver until you have a long straight stretch of road ahead that is clear of on-coming traffic.

111

Sometimes you will come upon a heavy truck struggling up a long hill, backing up traffic behind. The driver may attempt to signal you past though the way is blind from your vantage point. (Because truck cabs are higher off the ground, visibility is better than in automobiles.) By blinking his lights or turn signals or waving his arm, he may try to communicate to you that the coast is clear. Despite his thoughtfulness, it is best to ignore his signals unless their meaning is *unmistakable*. Many drivers have driven into head-on crashes because they misunderstood a trucker's signal. There is no uniform code to transmit this sort of information, so be extremely skeptical.

If you are traveling slower than the automobile behind, move over and give him every opportunity to pass. Though it shouldn't be intended as any sort of signal, a friendly wave of the arm indicates to the driver that you are aware of his intentions and will stay out of his way. If he chooses to pass with traffic approaching, be sure your automobile is under control. Should he have to cut in quickly, he may force you to take evasive action, so be prepared.

There are those individuals who, either consciously or unconsciously, apply more throttle as they are being passed. Tricks of this sort are boorish and completely inexcusable. Maintain a steady speed in this situation. Don't slow radically because you may have other automobiles running close behind.

The driver who habitually trails a few feet off the

Keep your eye on the crest of a hill during the approach and while you are climbing it. This will permit you to spot any danger ahead at the earliest possible moment. In this drawing the driver is about to sight a slow-moving tractor and wagon on the other side of the hill. This potential danger could just as well be a car passing illegally from the opposite direction, a stray cow, playing children, a stalled car, etc. It is a good idea to exercise caution when approaching and passing farm machinery that is chugging along the side of the road. In many states persons who do not have a driver's license, and even small children, are allowed to operate tractors for short distances on the highway. Few of these machines are equipped with rear-view mirrors or any signal lights whatsoever.

next car's bumper is known as a tailgater. The danger of this type of driving is obvious and most states forbid its practice. If you should find one of these individuals on your tail, slow down and let him by. The tailgater is a driver possessing poor judgment and it's much better to have an incompetent of this sort ahead of you, where you can keep an eye on him, rather than behind, where he may hit you.

If you should have the misfortune to get trapped in the left lane, always cut right, even if it means sideswiping the car you are trying to pass. Taking refuge on the left shoulder is not advised because this may be the exact spot where the oncoming car is heading. Keep in mind that a head-on collision is to be avoided at all costs.

Collisions of this type are common in passing situations. Nine out of ten are directly attributable to driver error. As you spend more time on the road, you will see drivers pull out to pass in the most dangerous places: on blind hills and curves, at intersections, over solid lines, etc. The moment may arrive when you will be driving around that blind curve or over that hilltop just as someone is trying such an insane move. When traveling over a hill, keep your eyes focused on the center of the road, right at the crest. This will give you the earliest possible sight of traffic in either lane. On a blind curve focus on the point at which you can see farthest around the bend. In both instances check the condition and width of the shoulder because you may have to use it on a second's notice.

Whenever the road goes out of sight, it is wise to ease back on the throttle slightly and prepare yourself for the unexpected. Even if you know the way blindfolded, take this precaution because you have no idea what sort of obstacle may be blocking your way. After all, a stray cow can weigh as much as a small sedan.

Should you be driving in unfamiliar territory, an indication of where the road is going can be gained from landmarks. If, for example, a row of power poles is bordering the highway, they may give you a suggestion of where the road goes over the hill before you can see the actual surface. Tops of power poles that stick above ground fog or drifting snow can also be handy for direction finding. Use landmarks as aids

Though they should never be relied upon exclusively, landmarks can be helpful in giving clues to the roadway ahead. Note how the utility poles indicate the radius of the blind curve ahead. Landmarks are a valid driving aid, because with an idea of which way the road will turn, you can devote most of your attention to the traffic that is liable to appear abruptly over the crest. This curve also has negative camber, meaning that it slopes to the outside rather than to the inside of the turn.

Notice in this picture that the line in the opposite lane is broken, permitting cars in that lane to pass even though the hill is blind. Everyone, including highway planners and workers, can make mistakes, so never place complete reliance on road markings.

but never rely on them. Keep your speed reduced until you see the road itself.

When traveling on main highways, you will find the road surface may change periodically. One county may choose to pave the surface with macadam while its neighbors will surface the same road with concrete.

When you spot a change in road surface, ease up until you determine its composition: It may be extraordinarily rough, meaning that your springs and shock absorbers will take a heavy buffeting if you arrive at too high a speed. At other boundaries there is a pronounced difference in the elevation of the highway, which can knock an automobile out of control if the driver is not alert.

There is little to choose between modern concrete and macadam roads. Both provide smooth, safe driving surfaces. However, as they age, both become more hazardous. Macadam will crumble and form deep potholes that can damage tires and hamper control of the automobile. Most concrete roads contain separations every twenty or thirty feet called expansion joints. Another joint divides the two lanes. When the road is new, these joints are unnoticeable. But as the road bed settles, these separations rise, causing the rhythmic thump-thump of the tires as you travel along. On roads of this type beware of the expansion joint in the middle of the highway. If the wheels brush against this, it may cause the car to lurch to the right. Cases have been recorded where this caused the automobile to go out of control.

Highways that have recently been covered with a layer of crushed stone deserve caution. Each pebble can act like a tiny ball bearing under spinning tires, so don't try to stop or turn fast on this type of surface.

Secondary roads of dirt or tar composition are nor-

Whenever the road goes out of sight, it is wise to ease off on the throttle slightly and prepare yourself for the unexpected. This is a fine example of a highly treacherous bend in the road. The shrubbery and weeds at the right reduce visibility and make the other end of the turn an unknown quantity. Also the hue of the pavement immediately ahead is darker, which means that a fresh coat of asphalt has recently been laid in your lane. This section of roadway may be much more slippery than the surface you are on. Remember that loss of control on a right-hand turn is likely to send you into the opposite lane. Buildings usually mean people, so prepare yourself for activity around the barn in the background.

mally narrow and bumpy. Unless they are in an excellent state of repair, normal highway speeds should never be attempted on these roads.

Caution should also be exercised if you are forced to use the dirt or gravel shoulder of a highway. These areas are often rutted and bumpy and can easily lurch the automobile into a spin. This danger is magnified if rain has transformed the dirt to mud.

Never cut sharply onto the shoulder. Try to turn the automobile gently, at a low speed. If you have no other choice (as in avoiding an accident) and must drive onto the shoulder at a higher than desired speed, watch for spin. The right wheels, as they hit the ruts or mud, may grab, sending the automobile into a skid to the left. Be ready to correct this tendency if you are involved in such a situation.

Some highways have a pronounced ridge between the road surface and the shoulder. If your right wheels happen to drop over that ledge, *slow down* before trying to steer back onto the road. If you attempt this at high speeds, you will have to steer sharply to the left to get the right wheels over the ridge. And once you return to the pavement, you will be steering diagonally across the road. In trying to get the automobile straightened out, you may begin a nasty skid.

Railroad grade crossings have been the scenes of countless tragic accidents. Even crossings where approaching trains are visible for several miles in each direction have taken their toll. As you near a railroad, slow down until you are sure the tracks are clear, never placing complete faith in any automatic signaling devices that may be installed. Never gamble your life on whether or not a complicated electronic signal

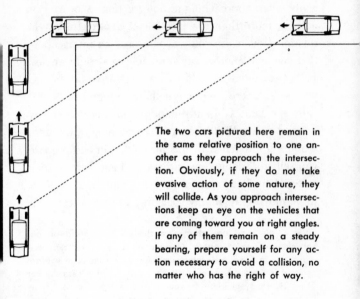

The two cars pictured here remain in the same relative position to one another as they approach the intersection. Obviously, if they do not take evasive action of some nature, they will collide. As you approach intersections keep an eye on the vehicles that are coming toward you at right angles. If any of them remain on a steady bearing, prepare yourself for any action necessary to avoid a collision, no matter who has the right of way.

will work—particularly when only a few seconds of travel time are at stake.

When slowing for rough sections of highway, such as a railroad crossing or the beginning of a detour, try to complete your braking before your wheels hit the rough surface. If the wheels begin to bounce while the brakes are on, they will lock up instantly, making control difficult. Most important, treat any potentially dangerous area with respect and have your automobile well under control before you arrive.

Though it is a seafarer's tool, the concept of relative bearings can be extremely handy to the driver, especially when approaching an intersection. A bearing is nothing more than the position of another object in relation to you. Imagine, as you near an intersection, that you spot another car approaching at right angles. If that car seems to hold the same relative position as you near the crossing, you will arrive together. Nautically speaking, you and the other car are on a steady bearing or a collision course. By watching other automobiles approach with this in mind, you can prepare yourself for dangerous situations long before they materialize. If a car coming from your right appears to be moving, relatively speaking, to your left, it will

Forks in the road are always treacherous and should be approached with extra caution. Never depend on the vehicles coming at you to signal their intentions, especially if the road you are entering is a main highway. In the situation pictured here the car at the right may pull into the road ahead of you or cross directly in front of you to enter the lane at the left. If you were the driver of the car at the right, you should be on the lookout for cars darting into your lane from your left side.

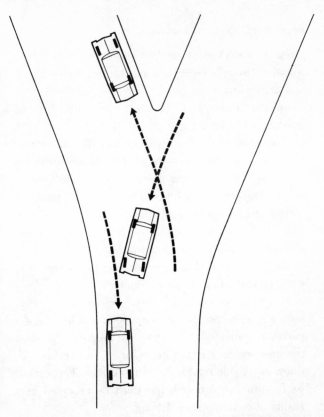

In this diagram the most hazardous position is occupied by the second car from the bottom, because it could have gotten into trouble with either of the other two vehicles. Forks where one of the roads is a main highway and the other is a secondary route are particularly bad. For example, if the road forking to the left were a secondary road and the one to the right a main road, the car at the top of the drawing would have had to cut across the main flow of traffic. By the same token the car at the bottom has had to cut diagonally into the primary flow of traffic, possibly without benefit of traffic signals or warning signs.

probably reach the intersection before you. If it moves relatively to your right, or tends to drop behind, you will arrive first.

Relative bearings are like landmarks: use them as aids, not as foolproof guides.

Treat forks in the road with respect. Because traffic moves in three directions the chances of accidents are multiplied. At a fork in the road, keep this rule in mind: Use *extreme* caution if you have to cross, or merge with, other lanes of traffic. Unless an intersection of this nature is equipped with a signal light, also use maximum care when making a left turn.

The fascination of highway driving lies in the wide variety of situations to be encountered.

Traveling on most first-class American highways with a safe, responsive automobile is a delightful experience, provided the driver is prepared to meet the unexpected. Around every curve, over every hill, down every side road is potential danger. This cannot be forgotten or ignored, but must be accepted as a reality of contemporary driving.

Never be frightened of driving. If it scares you, stay home. You will surely be involved in an accident if you let fear govern your actions behind the wheel.

Respect driving as something that demands a definite responsibility to yourself and your fellow citizens. By shouldering this responsibility, you will then find that driving can become what it should be, a wonderful twentieth-century activity.

10

THE DECEPTIVE TURNPIKES

A little more than twenty years ago, the 1939 New York World's Fair was attracting worldwide attention with its exciting and imaginative displays. Over a period of two years, thousands of people flocked to the fair to view elaborate exhibitions from almost every nation and major industry on earth.

One of the highlights was an enormous model landscape of the future U.S.A. In that representation, skyscrapers, all glass and steel, poked into the sky. Criss-crossing the earth were hundreds of super-highways, with six and eight lanes, complete with complicated cloverleafs and access roads.

In 1939–40 that model looked like something that might be found on Venus. Yet today glass and steel skyscrapers and super-highways are commonplace. Our world has advanced at a whirlwind pace in recent years, bringing new conveniences to everyone. The driver of today, for example, can travel great distances on super-highways at cruising speeds only slightly below the absolute *maximum* of the average 1940 automobile! If someone had predicted then that Americans would soon be able to travel from New York City to Chicago without hitting a traffic light, he would have been regarded as some sort of lunatic. Today that can be done with ease.

But the arrival of super-highways, referred to as turnpikes, thruways, expressways, freeways, etc., depending on their locale, have also added new challenges and hazards to driving.

Probably the development of a false sense of security is the most dangerous thing that can happen to a driver on a super-highway. Many people view roads of this type as thoroughfares where accidents never happen. This attitude behind the wheel means concentration has been seriously reduced.

Because no traffic can enter from side roads and vehicles traveling in opposite directions are separated by grass or concrete malls, the chances for accidents are lessened, but they still occur with alarming regularity. Incidents in which automobiles race out of control across the center mall and smash head-on into approaching traffic are not uncommon. Some accidents of this nature are caused by mechanical failure, others by the driver's dozing off. Numerous one-car accidents in which the car plunges off the road into a bridge abutment or a fence post can also be blamed on sleeping drivers. Collisions between a passing car and one whipping out of the right-hand lane are also common.

In less than a decade, many of our super-highways have made the transition from the brand-new roomy arteries they were to overcrowded, obsolete nightmares. The freeways that lace Los Angeles are often more crowded and more dangerous than the old-fashioned streets they replaced. This heavy usage of many of our super-highways has reduced their margin of safety, meaning that more attention to driving, not less, is necessary.

As you find yourself motoring along a spacious super-highway, the natural thing is to relax. The newer automobiles hold a legal 60–65 mph speed with little effort or noise. With no shifting or braking and a minimum of steering necessary, it can become quite difficult to keep your mind on your driving.

It is easy enough to say here, "Keep alert on the turnpikes," and it's easy enough for you, now far away from the highway, to agree. But after a few hours on a straight, wide-open stretch of road, it may be hard to maintain that alertness.

A basic rule of turnpike driving is to break up the trip with frequent stops. Try to get out from behind the wheel every hundred miles. Never, under any circumstances, drive more than two hours without interruption. Long stints behind the wheel can be extremely fatiguing, making you all the more prone to boredom and drowsiness. Stopping does not necessarily have to involve a leisurely cup of coffee. A brief walk in the fresh air will do wonders for your alertness.

Be sure your seating position is correct. Driving in an unnatural posture will cut circulation more rapidly on a turnpike because leg and arm movement for steering, braking, etc., is limited. Some people find their throttle foot goes to sleep after an hour or so on a turnpike. This can be traced to a seating position which is restricting normal blood circulation. Wiggling their toes is a measure many race drivers use in distance races to correct a sleeping foot or leg.

Switching feet on the throttle is *not* recommended. This can create an awful tangle should you have to make an emergency stop. If your foot goes to sleep, stop at the first rest area; it's a good indication that you need a break. Massaging the thigh and calf while you are stopped will help this condition.

Stale air in an automobile can cause sleepiness, so be sure you keep a window open. This flow of fresh air through the car will help keep you alert. If the weather is chilly, don't run the heater full power. Warmth, like stale air, induces sleep. Adjust the temperature so it is a few degrees below that which would be absolutely comfortable.

On occasion, all the precautions in the world will not prevent you from becoming sleepy. Most turnpike regulations forbid cars from parking on the shoulder, so you must press on until you reach a specified area before resting. If you feel drowsy, roll the windows down and drive with the fresh air rushing in. Adjust the wind wing to direct a blast of air square in your face. If this does not help, stop your car *well off* the shoulder and get out for a second. Walk around the car once or twice to stretch your muscles. If snow is on the ground, rub some on your face. Then drive on to the nearest service area.

When you do stop, make a point of washing your hands, wrists, face and the back of your neck with cold water. This coolness will refresh and stimulate you. Then, after a steaming cup of coffee or tea, you should be ready for the road once again.

Don't eat heavily in situations like this. While the body is digesting food, sleepiness comes more easily. Chewing gum is recommended as are chocolate bars, which provide dextrose for quick energy. *Never* resort to artificial stimulants such as anti-sleep pills. These drugs can play havoc with your reflexes.

Should you find yourself too sleepy to continue even after stopping, nap in your car, but only do this in warm weather. Sleeping in their car in the winter tempts many people to leave the engine running to provide heat. You stand a chance of never waking from a sleep like this. Without the airstream caused by movement, carbon-monoxide fumes will rise into the car's interior from any leaks in the exhaust system. The alternative of sleeping without heat can also be disastrous. If the outside temperature is well below freezing, 15 degrees and under, the cold quickly penetrates the light insulation of an automobile. A person sleeping in these surroundings can freeze to death. Heater on or off, cold-weather snoozing in a car is not wise.

Super-highways have a minimum of two lanes in

each direction. Slower cars are supposed to run to the inside or the right, faster cars to the left. If this rule was universally observed, turnpike driving would be simplified considerably.

Stay right unless passing. Remain clear of faster traffic, permitting it to pass in normal fashion to your left. Unless traffic is extremely light, you will find yourself forced into frequent passing situations on a turnpike. You may be running at the legal limit, say 60 mph, in the right-hand lane. This is fine until you overtake some traffic traveling at 50–55 mph. You move into the passing lane, only to be immediately overtaken by traffic running illegally at 70 mph. Where do you go? The right lane is packed with slower-moving cars, the left with speeders. The best solution is to continue at the legal limit until you have passed the slower traffic, then pull back into the right lane to let the faster cars pass. Though you have no right to hold up the people behind even though they are breaking the law, neither should you feel obligated to scurry out of their way. Provided you are running as quickly as legally possible, you have every right to use the left lane to pass slower automobiles. Exercise that privilege but not at the expense of creating a bottleneck or cutting off another driver. If other people are imprudent enough to drive faster than they should, let them go. Drive for yourself—and keep to the right whenever possible.

Many problems would be solved if everyone drove

Wide expanses of four-lane highways such as this seem perfectly harmless, but many serious accidents are recorded annually on these roads. Unless you are passing (as shown here), remain in the right lane. Despite the confidence it inspires, the double line separating the traffic is not an invisible shield, and head-on collisions are not impossible. Never let your guard down merely because you are on a four-lane highway.

at the legal limit. Speed would be equalized and passing would be cut to a minimum. That is too much to hope for. You won't travel far on a turnpike before you come upon some individual blithely cruising down the left lane 5–10 mph under the speed limit.

Why these people refuse to drive to the right is a

mystery. Possibly some are acting as unofficial speed regulators, holding up those who want to drive faster. More than likely, though, people who remain in the outer lane have let their concentration lapse. They have been overcome by the false sense of security we mentioned earlier and are paying no attention whatsoever to what is going on around them.

How do you pass one of these drivers? Do you race up behind and blast your horn until he moves over? Or do you ignore him and wiggle by on his right? Neither procedure is correct. The first is rude and impolite and may anger the driver, making him all the more obstinate. Passing on the right is *never* wise on a turnpike (or anywhere else besides intersections, for that matter). Whenever you resort to this tactic, you leave yourself wide open to be sideswiped by the car on the left. As you are sneaking by, the other driver may suddenly realize his error and turn into your path. The fact that he probably has a blind spot to his right (most cars do) makes you doubly vulnerable.

The recommended way to pass a driver in the left lane is to warn him with a light tap on the horn. If this does not work, wait a few moments and repeat. This should be enough for most drivers and they will move over. If further measures are necessary, blink your lights. Day or night, he should get the idea when he spots the light in his mirror. Sometimes nothing short of dropping a bomb will get one of these types out of the way. If this is the case, *do not* trail behind. Get over into the right lane, reduce speed and wait for the situation to clear. By remaining in the left lane, you are only adding to the bottleneck, so get out of the way.

When you overtake slower cars and trucks, be sure that you allow ample room for passing or cutting speed. Don't get into the position where you are bearing down on slower traffic and, just as you prepare to pass, another car looms up behind you in the left lane. If you are going too fast, you may have to slam on your brakes to keep from overrunning the vehicles ahead. It should be mentioned that if you are forced to use your brakes in normal turnpike travel you are probably overdriving. If you leave the proper margin, brake application should be absolutely unnecessary (disregarding emergency situations, exiting, etc.).

Before you attempt to pass, check the traffic behind. Use your side mirror to make sure that the left lane is clear. If a car is overtaking you, don't try to race him around the vehicles ahead. That automobile has the right of way, and you are breaking the law if you cut into his lane. Back off, let him pass, then pass the cars ahead.

The remainder of the passing sequence should be carried out as it would be on a regular highway. Be sure to use your turn signals. Watch for cars cutting into your lane should you attempt to pass a string of slower automobiles.

131

Buzzing along at turnpike speeds, you can find yourself in very close quarters without warning. While passing slower cars watch the cars ahead in the inner lane too. In this instance the driver of the truck may suddenly decide to pull out to pass, blocking the path for both you and the car immediately in front.

Try to stay clear of other automobiles. This should be a keynote of your turnpike driving. When you are able to run for long periods of time at a steady speed without forcing others to take abnormal steering or braking action to avoid you, you will be an accomplished turnpike driver.

Many people writing on the subject of super-highway driving have recommended that speeds be varied periodically. This, they say, will help overcome boredom. We cannot agree. A driver would have to add or subtract a minimum of 10–15 mph before any real impression of a speed change became apparent. Alterations of this magnitude would mean an erratic, unsafe and uneconomical trip.

Smoothness is essential in all driving, and on the turnpike a steady speed is an important step toward smoothness. Because your movements are more predictable to other drivers, you will be driving more safely. Your automobile will function better at a steady speed and will provide better gas mileage. And we cannot help wondering which driver would be more bored: the person who is concentrating on maintaining an exact speed or the one who is casually lurching along at a variety of velocities.

The relatively higher speeds and generally longer trips on turnpikes result in numerous mechanical troubles. A heavy percentage of lame automobiles can be found on most super-highways. Normally the difficulties center around broken fan belts, water hoses, flat tires, blown gaskets, etc.—failures that are stimulated by sustained high speeds. Though turnpike driving is easier on your engine than stop-start city driving, parts like those mentioned above may fail faster. If you are planning a trip via super-highway, have your automobile's running gear checked before you leave. A breakdown on a turnpike is generally more expensive and more time consuming than one that occurs elsewhere.

If you should have a mechanical failure, be sure to get your automobile well off the roadway when you stop. In the event you are approaching a turnpike bridge or viaduct when your car begins to act up, stop *before* reaching it. Turnpike bridges, viaducts, and ramps do not have shoulders, meaning your car will be blocking a lane of traffic should it come to a halt.

A driver can easily become acclimated to speeds of 60 mph and over on a turnpike. Relatively speaking, 40 mph seems like a slow walk. When you exit a super-highway, remember that the speed limit may be lowered. A normal tendency will be to continue at turnpike speeds. Resist this temptation, because you are back in the old world of traffic again—the same old world people drove in long before the 1939 New York World's Fair.

11

DRIVING AT NIGHT
AND IN BAD WEATHER

One foolproof answer exists to the question of how to drive in adverse weather—*don't.* If you can, stay off the roads when conditions are not ideal.

Actually, driving in bad weather is not so dangerous as it might seem. It would appear logical for accident statistics to skyrocket in direct proportion to the adversity of the elements, but serious accidents often decrease when driving conditions drop below par. Why? Because drivers tend to pay more attention. The person who habitually drives one-handed, gazing serenely at the countryside, generally comes to and operates at full effort when the weather gets poor. One cannot help but wonder how much the accident rate would dip if people drove as intently in pleasant weather as they do when it is raining or snowing.

Adverse driving conditions reduce either visibility or control, and in some instances, such as rain or snow, both are cut down.

By considering clear, windless, daylight hours as the only really perfect conditions for driving, we can validly describe both dusk and night as adverse periods for highway travel. However, because these periods occur every day, many people tend to take

Cloudy or rainy weather greatly reduces visibility. Objects ahead are blended together until you get dangerously close. Here two boys are walking on the wrong side of the highway, with their backs to traffic, and their clothing has little or no contrast with the slope in the background. The approaching automobile gives you nowhere to go should the pair wander onto the road, so sound your horn as a warning and slow down until you have passed them.

them for granted and fail to adjust their driving accordingly.

In an average twenty-four-hour day, dusk is the most dangerous time for driving. This period is characterized by a dull half light without sharp shadows. Everything blends together, making objects difficult to see and distances hard to judge. Similar lighting conditions occur at dawn but are less hazardous for the driver, because, driving from night into day, his eyes are more acclimated to darkness. Additionally, dawn finds traffic activity at a near minimum, whereas dusk often arrives at the height of the rush hour.

During these marginal light periods, every driver

should have his headlights on. But many content themselves with their parking lights, while others do not bother with any illumination until total darkness sets in. You have to be ready for this in the dusk, so drive with maximum alertness. People will make the wildest sort of maneuvers in front of you on the assumption that they can be seen—even if they are in a dull gray car without lights.

Though there is little that can be done about the other fellow, except to avoid him, you can at least make sure that you will be seen. Don't settle for parking lights. They are intended only for what their name implies. When the sun goes down, snap on your headlights (low beam), and you will be sure to be seen.

With the coming of complete darkness, visibility actually improves slightly. Approaching automobiles can often be detected at a greater distance than in daylight. For example, a car coming from behind a hill reveals itself by its light beams, whereas it would be invisible by day.

You will notice that a moment of complete blindness occurs just as an approaching automobile darts past. The brightness of the lights, immediately followed by darkness, forces your eyes to make an instantaneous adjustment. Imagine the other car's lights as a curtain. For all you know, the road can be littered with obstacles behind that curtain. Be sure that you are prepared to take emergency action as you move into this blind area.

137

A good driver should make it a habit to switch on his low beams whenever he is approaching or overtaking traffic. The glare of high-beam headlights in a driver's eyes or in his rear-view mirror can radically reduce his vision. For the sake of self-preservation, be sure to lower your lights for approaching traffic. After all, the driver you blind may wander into your lane and hit you head-on.

An effective passing signal can be made by flickering your lights as you overtake a slower car. Before you pull out to pass, flick on your high beams for an instant. This will indicate to the driver ahead that you are passing. Many drivers will courteously answer your signal by flicking their high beams off as an unofficial go-ahead sign. Once you have passed, return to your high beams.

Besides blurring the driver's view of conditions ahead, rain can make a highway slippery, increasing stopping distances and the danger of skidding.

The first half hour of a rainstorm is the most dangerous. During this period the rainwater combines with the oil and rubber on the pavement surface, making a microscopic film rivaling ice for slipperiness. After approximately thirty minutes; the volumes of water will wash the surface clean, cutting down (but by no means eliminating) the glaze. Treat this initial period in a rainstorm as critical.

Even after the pavement has been bathed almost clean, it will still remain more slippery than when dry. Because tire adhesion has been cut, handling will be affected. Expect any bad habits your automobile has to be exaggerated in wet weather. If it tends toward oversteer, that condition will increase in the rain. This, coupled with the fact that less steering control is available on slippery surfaces, means your automobile will go out of control easier and will be more difficult to correct. All braking, steering and acceleration must be done with finesse in the rain. Make a conscious effort toward smoothness, trying to avoid sudden changes of speed or direction.

In the autumn of the year, falling leaves will coat the highways. When these get wet, they make very slippery footing for an automobile. Beware!

Be sure that your windshield wipers are in good condition. Nothing can place a more immediate handicap on a driver in the rain than a smeared, water-streaked windshield. If the water does not wipe off cleanly but forms into small beads, chances are someone has cleaned the window with an oily rag. Rather than try to see through this mess, stop and wipe the surface with a rag or handkerchief. (If the condition is serious, stop and sluice the windshield with a bottle of cola. This will do wonders.)

Night driving, coupled with rain, forms one of the most common extremely dangerous driving situations. Added to the poor visibility is the problem of reflections from the pavement. The lights of oncoming automobiles will dance on the water-soaked road, blurring and distorting the view to a point where no accurate judgments can be made. Driving at night in the rain should be avoided by beginning drivers whenever possible.

Fog can blanket an area at the most unexpected moments. It may engulf a driver for a matter of seconds on an otherwise clear night as he passes a low spot in the road; he may encounter it with rain, with snow, in the summer or the winter, in the mountains or on the seacoast. Fog is nothing more than a low-lying cloud. Though certain seaboard areas are fogbound regularly, don't be surprised to find this condition anywhere in the United States outside of the arid Southwest.

Fog alone will not seriously reduce tire adhesion, but of course it will cut visibility. If you encounter fog, pare your speed and turn on your low beams, *day or night*. Though brighter, the light of the high beams is diffused upward into the murk, making the scene even more blurred. The solid center line may be the only tangible landmark to follow but fight this temptation. Try to drive by the right shoulder of the road (made much easier in the states which have painted stripes on the roadsides) where you will be away from oncoming traffic. If you use the center line as a guide, you will have an unconscious tendency to steer your car down the middle of the road. This can be fatal even when the weather is clear.

Ground fog is a special hazard that will often be

encountered on cold, clear nights. It usually lurks in dips and ravines where the driver will unwittingly meet it after zooming over the crest of a hill. If you should plunge into ground fog, snap on your low beams and slow down. Normally the view will clear within a few hundred yards. But remember, if you have encountered it once, there is a good chance you will hit it again. If you follow the rule of easing up a bit every time the road goes out of sight, you will be much better prepared for this hazard.

When the temperature hovers near the freezing point, the danger of freezing rain or sleet arises. This occurs when rain lands on the cold road surface and forms into ice. This condition not only makes controlling the automobile a delicate operation but can reduce visibility by freezing over windows, side mirrors and headlight lenses.

A word of caution should be injected here about keeping headlights clear. When driving in sleet or snow, a heavy layer of ice may slowly form over the lights, reducing the beam range and power. This process may be so gradual that the driver will be unaware of the change. If you are driving in wet weather of any type, periodically wipe your headlights clean; you will be amazed at how visibility will improve.

Don't be lulled into believing that ice can materialize on the highway only when the temperature is below freezing. Often the earth is colder than the air, causing rain to freeze despite the fact that the weatherman says it is no colder than 33–34 degrees.

Whenever the thermometer is hovering near 32 degrees, be on the lookout for ice—even if the pavement is bare. Any water on the road will freeze in these conditions, forming a small ice rink on an otherwise dry highway.

Many wintry highways will contain patches of ice. Possibly 75 percent of the road will be clear, while the remainder will be icy. Try to do all of your controlling on the dry areas. Should you suddenly roll onto an icy stretch cross it *without* changing speed or direction. If you must brake, make heavy applications *up to* the edge of the ice. (By now you should be well aware of the dangers of braking on a slippery surface.)

In areas with a heavy snowfall, a daytime thaw may melt the highway ice but the lower nighttime temperatures may glaze the road with another solid coating. Added to this may be a layer of fresh snow that completely obscures the slippery areas.

If you are paying attention, you should be able to sense immediately that you have ice under your wheels. Because friction between the roadway and the front tires is lessened, steering will become feather light. You will feel the rear tires lose their solid grip on the pavement and begin queasy little movements to the right and left. *Make no harsh movements on ice.* Stay off the brakes if at all possible, using them only with gentle on-off applications should a serious situation arise.

Rainy or icy pavement also accentuates a car's bad habits. If your automobile tends toward understeer, it will probably plow ahead in the face of a turn until the wheels are cocked to near full lock. The danger then arises that the front wheels will gain adhesion, whipping the tail around in a wild skid.

Steer to the left or right and the car will be inclined to slide straight head on the turned wheels. Slam on the brakes and it will skid onward almost as quickly as before. A quick burst of speed will cause the driving wheels to lose their grip and spin helplessly. Let us amend the rule we stated above: *Make no harsh movements on ice because they are absolutely useless.*

Making an emergency stop on ice is an extremely difficult task. The best possibility is to search out an area on the roadside that may not be so slippery. Oftentimes the shoulder is frozen but rough, making it a better surface for the tires to grip. A shoulder banked with snow forms excellent resistance so don't hesitate to take refuge there.

By keeping the speed of your automobile cut back, you should eliminate to a large degree the need for lusty braking or steering. Keep in mind that the faster you go the farther you slide.

Much has been written about getting up a hill when the road is covered with ice. The secret to making such a maneuver, apparently, is to eliminate wheel spin at all costs. This is true, to a certain point. And in reality that point lies about halfway up the hill. Here the driver, carefully creeping along so as not to spin the wheels, finds the pull of gravity overcoming the momentum of his car. Speed will fall off until the car finally comes to a halt, its wheels rotating helplessly. Getting up an icy hill requires a good head start. If you don't have enough momentum at the bottom, you will not make it, wheel spin or no wheel spin. As you approach a slippery hill, try to muster as much speed as is safely possible. Keep enough power on to maintain speed but not so much as to break traction. Some wheel spin may occur, but this will not be disastrous unless headway begins to lessen. Should your forward movement stop, you have no choice but to back down and try again. But if you have a couple of passengers on board, their pushing may provide just enough extra thrust to get you to the top.

Without question the most slippery roads develop when a cold rain is falling on an icy surface. Water on top of ice forms the most dangerous wintertime highway condition. A person has trouble keeping his footing, much less trying to drive an automobile across the surface. *Creep* while driving on icy pavements in the rain because you are in one of the most treacherous highway environments conceivable.

Like rain, snow hinders both visibility and control. It comes in many forms: in light, fluffy flakes; in fat,

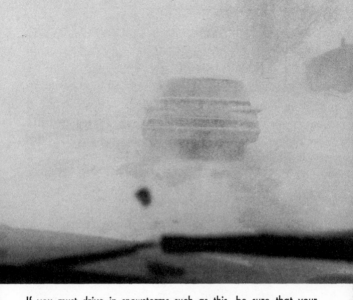

If you must drive in snowstorms such as this, be sure that your lights are on. The car ahead, though only a few yards away, is almost invisible. If its taillights were on, it would be much easier to spot.

wet globs that tend to clog windshield wipers; and in tiny, wind-driven pellets that quickly pile high drifts across the road.

Keep in mind that packed snow on the road can become as slippery as ice, especially if it has undergone steady polishing from passing automobiles. Also remember that snow may cover patches of ice. Exercise the same caution as if you were driving on ice.

Heavy snowstorms hamper visibility as much as fog. And the same method of correction is recommended.

Keep your lights on low beam and stop periodically to clean off your driving and taillights. Snow, especially the wet, heavy variety, will build up at an amazing rate.

When the wind blows, drifts form. Wherever there is a roadside obstacle, such as a slope or a fence, drifts will build up. Where the wind has a clear sweep of the road, the surface may be almost bare.

During blizzards, road crews may not be able to keep the thoroughfares clear, and you may have to breach drifts two or three feet deep (much deeper than that, and the cause is nearly hopeless). The most important part of running through a drift is hitting it square. If the wheels are cocked, the automobile will sheer off and become bogged down. Drive straight into the barrier with steady power on. The initial impact may toss snow over the hood, cutting visibility for a second, but don't lose heart.

Should you come upon a deep drift, stop and check the situation before ramming through. Another car may be stuck there and your blind surge may cause a serious collision. And yet by stopping you are running the risk of being hit from behind by another automobile, so there is no clear-cut answer.

Moments like this make travel in a blizzard the most demanding and fatiguing challenge facing a driver. When you encounter such conditions, the best thing to do is to find a motel or hotel and hole up until the weather clears. If that is impossible, move ahead *slowly*, trying to keep a steady speed. Be on the lookout for automobiles everywhere—heading in the wrong direction, stuck at weird angles across the road, etc.

Wind direction and velocity may have a great deal to do with your progress. For example, making headway to the north or south when the wind direction is from the east or west is generally impossible because you are running at right angles to the wind and drifts. A trip against the wind would be almost as futile. With the wind behind you, conditions might be slightly better, but no radical difference should be expected.

A final note about drifting: it does not have to be snowing for deep drifts to form. A brisk wind on a clear, starlit night can build up deep drifts merely

Though it may not be snowing, wind may whip light, fluffy snow around to a point where visibility is seriously reduced. If you look closely at this picture, a car can be seen up ahead near the tree by the roadside.

Dark, granulated snow covering a road means that sand or salt mixtures have been applied to improve traction.

by blowing around the snow that is already on the ground. If the snow is deep along the roadside, be on the lookout for an occasional drift when the wind is blowing.

Countless tempers have been lost, fingers frost-bitten and automobiles ruined trying to get free of the clutches, of snow. One of the best precautions against getting stuck is proper tires. Conventional tires with plenty of tread or even better the special snow tires available everywhere are a prerequisite to winter driving. Without traction, you will go nowhere in the snow.

Should you become stuck, try the rocking technique mentioned in Chapter 5. Do not overdo this if you

In snowy weather be on the alert for cars parked in all sorts of unusual places. Because of a high bank of snow to the left, the driver of the car on the right has parked it in a very dangerous spot.

seem to make no headway. You may be grinding a hole in the snow (by melting from frictional heat) with your spinning wheels. This of course only makes getting out more difficult. If rocking does not work, *stop*, and get out and look the situation over. It may be that thirty seconds expended to clear away some snow will get you free. Most important, *don't* sit behind the wheel racing the engine and spinning the wheels. Usually one person pushing will do wonders, so put any passengers you have to work immediately.

Anyone who lives in a climate where heavy snow can be expected should add certain equipment to his automobile. A husky snow shovel is essential. A bag of sand or salt for application under the rear wheels will also be useful. (If carried in the trunk, its added weight will provide extra ballast for the rear wheels, too.)

Carry flares. When you become bogged down in an area where you may be hit by other traffic, set out flares fore and aft. A light 10–20-foot length of tow line will also be handy should you have to be towed by another car.

Tire chains have dropped out of vogue for use in snow. With the advent of special tires, many people abandoned chains because they were hard to mount and made an unholy noise on dry pavement. But if you expect to be driving in snowy or icy weather, though this should be avoided if at all possible, carry reinforced chains in your trunk. Then, if the road surface gets dangerously slippery, you can stop at a service station and put the chains on. Though they have their drawbacks, chains hold an undeniable advantage over snow tires in heavy going.

If you reside in an area where winter weather is bad, purchase a car with a limited-slip differential. This device assures that both wheels will turn on slippery pavement. You may have noticed that a car with one rear wheel on ice and the other on dry pavement will be immobile. The wheel in contact with the ice will spin uselessly while the other wheel—the one that would do some good—won't turn at all. This trouble is eliminated with a limited-slip, so get one if you can.

Watch out for cars stuck in the snow. They may be found in almost any position on the road. In this picture notice how the swirling snow ahead blends the road into the horizon, making it impossible to determine if there are six inches or six feet of snow covering the right of way.

Also be sure that your windshield defrosters are always in good working order. A foggy windshield will blend with the white landscape to make seeing where you are going a nightmare. Windshield washers should be employed in poor weather, especially when the snow is slushy, causing oncoming cars to toss melting snow and mud across your windshield.

Driving in foul weather is not much fun. In fact, it can be extremely hazardous, so, we repeat, *avoid it whenever possible*. Should it be necessary to drive, drive slowly, concentrating on smoothness and steadiness. Keep your eyes open at all times. With the help of the right equipment you probably then will be able to make the trip safely.

12

LAST CHANCE!

Even the most cautious and talented drivers are faced with the possibility of an accident. As the miles of driving steadily mount, the law of averages makes a mishap of some sort almost inevitable. The accident may be caused by the actions of another automobile, by a mechanical failure or possibly by a momentary lapse of judgment or attention. However, because of his driving skill, the expert may be able to minimize the damage. Where someone less prepared for such an event might be seriously injured, the good driver may escape with nothing more than some minor dents in his automobile.

By placing a few important rules in a cubbyhole of your mind, you too may someday be able to get out of a potentially disastrous situation without a scratch.

Avoid a head-on collision at all costs. Nothing in the realm of motoring is more lethal. A pair of automobiles colliding at 50 mph each would provide the same impact as if one slammed into a brick wall at 100 mph. A head-on crash is almost guaranteed to take lives. Keep yourself oriented toward the right side of the highway, away from oncoming traffic. If an emergency arises which forces you to change direction, your first reaction should be to turn right rather than left. If this means ramming a bridge abutment, do it if swinging left will result in a head-on collision. Any alternative this side of dropping off the edge of the Grand Canyon is preferable to a crash of this nature. This is why we warn you to pass carefully, to stay right in fog, to watch the crests of hills—because errors in these situations are likely to mean a smash-up with an approaching car.

Try to keep the car upright. A driver and his passengers are in trouble if the automobile turns over. Because the roofs of modern cars are not reinforced, they will collapse like bedsheets. All racing cars of today are equipped with roll bars, which prevent injury to the driver if his car rolls over. These stout tubular frameworks have saved countless men from serious injury. But the installation of roll bars in passenger cars would be useless unless everyone used seat belts (what's the use of keeping the roof intact if the passengers are going to be tossed out?). Hopefully, the day will arrive when seat belts are in universal use.

It is nearly impossible to flip an automobile by turning sharply. A car will simply spin unless its wheels hit something during the sideward movement to impede their progress. This might be compared to a person tripping. His body pitches forward when his foot gets caught. Likewise the body of the automobile tends to flop over if the outside wheels catch

153

on a curb, ditch, muddy shoulder, etc. The best remedy for this is to keep the automobile pointed straight ahead in emergency situations. If you are going to leave the road, attempt to make the exit nose first. This will help to keep the automobile upright and give you the best chance of regaining control. Saying this is one thing; accomplishing it as your automobile slews sideways down an icy highway is another. Getting the car pointed properly should be the *primary* consideration in this situation. Don't worry about stopping, signaling or anything else; just get the automobile back on course and the danger of flipping will diminish.

Don't give up if you lose control. Many serious accidents could be avoided if the drivers involved did not give up so easily. Too many people who feel their automobile go out from under them stop driving. Right there, when their efforts are needed most, they quit. Battle for control with everything you've got. Hold onto the wheel and fight! The automobile may have clipped off a dozen guardrails and bounced off two trees, but you still might be able to keep it clear of other obstacles. Remember, speed is falling off every second, and the longer you grapple for control the nearer to a full stop the automobile has come.

You will never regain control if you are not behind the steering wheel. The extreme forces that come to bear in a collision or a high-speed spin tend to rip you loose from your seat and send you flopping onto the pavement or around the inside of the car. Only a seat belt will keep you in position. A belt does double duty by keeping the driver where he belongs both *before* and *during* the moment of impact.

Before your driving days are over, you will probably feel an automobile skid. If you are able to maintain the right speeds in all the situations described in Chapter 11, the possibilities of such an occurrence will be reduced. But, not being endowed with flawless judgment, we all may get in over our heads occasionally. A skid can easily be corrected by steering in the direction in which the car is sliding. If the tail is sliding left, steer left; if it is going right, steer right. Because most cars you will drive basically understeer, a réduction of the throttle will also help. This will eliminate the chances of the front wheels sliding, and the tail should snap into line. The most dangerous part of a skid is overcorrection. For every person that crashes off the road because he did not control a skid enough, probably ten go off because they *overcorrected.* The instant they feel the tail of the car break loose, they crank the steering wheel over to correct. This in itself is all right, except that they correct too much, causing the tail to fishtail in the other direction. This skid in the opposite direction is met with another wild turn of the wheel, causing the rear end to wigwag a third time. Each time an automobile fishtails, the skids become more violent, making it progressively harder for the driver to regain control.

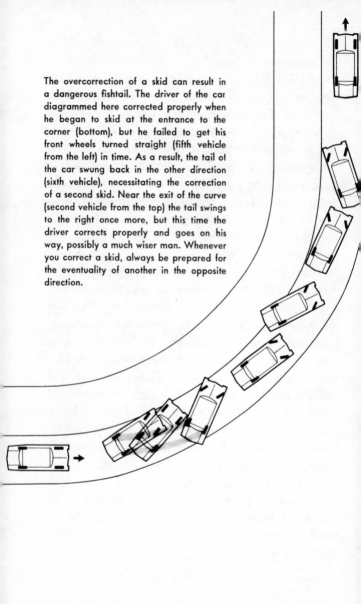

The overcorrection of a skid can result in a dangerous fishtail. The driver of the car diagrammed here corrected properly when he began to skid at the entrance to the corner (bottom), but he failed to get his front wheels turned straight (fifth vehicle from the left) in time. As a result, the tail of the car swung back in the other direction (sixth vehicle), necessitating the correction of a second skid. Near the exit of the curve (second vehicle from the top) the tail swings to the right once more, but this time the driver corrects properly and goes on his way, possibly a much wiser man. Whenever you correct a skid, always be prepared for the eventuality of another in the opposite direction.

Don't panic when you feel the skid begin. Turn the wheel gently at first, applying more lock if the slide persists. Be ready to correct in the opposite direction should a fishtail start. (The hand positions on the wheel recommended in Chapter 2 will be especially important here because they will provide the widest possible turning arc in either direction.) Overcorrection is especially easy on ice or wet roads because the wheels turn so easily. If possible, practice skid correction on a slippery parking lot or vacant area. Only by feeling the automobile "out of shape" will you perfect your correction methods.

A road does not have to be covered with ice, wet leaves, etc., for automobiles to go out of control. Each year many accidents occur on gentle, wide bends in the most ideal driving weather. The wreck is usually explained with such generalities as "he lost control" or "he was going too fast." Excessive speed is usually a factor, though the driver may not have been surpassing the legal limit. Specifically, the speed was excessive *for the conditions*. Forty miles an hour on a 20-mph curve can be more dangerous than 80 mph on a 60-mph curve.

One-car accidents involving a driver who simply crashes off a curve are wholly unnecessary. Normally a little judgment backed up by some driving know-how would have prevented the incident. You must provide the judgment, but we can provide a few clues on last-ditch efforts to keep your automobile under control on a curve.

157

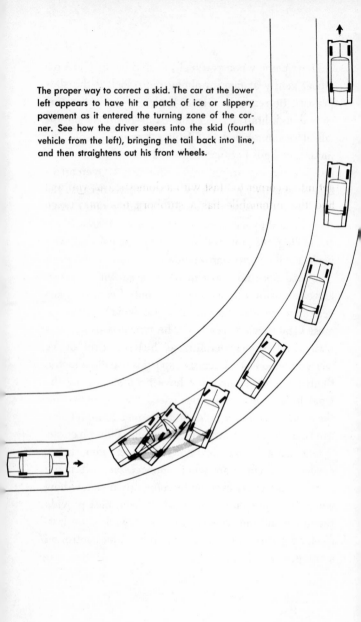

The proper way to correct a skid. The car at the lower left appears to have hit a patch of ice or slippery pavement as it entered the turning zone of the corner. See how the driver steers into the skid (fourth vehicle from the left), bringing the tail back into line, and then straightens out his front wheels.

As we have said, most American cars understeer. The front wheels of an understeering car, by nature of the design, slip before the rear. If the rear wheels slide on a slippery surface at lower speeds, reducing power will automatically bring the tail back into line.

If, through an error in judgment (which can happen to the best and most cautious of drivers), you should get into a corner too fast with a domestic car, you will find the automobile has a stubborn tendency to go straight ahead. The front wheels are slipping while the rear wheels are maintaining traction—and driving you straight ahead. Power in this situation will only add to the forward thrust and send you rocketing off the road. You must get off the throttle for an instant. This sudden slowdown will transfer weight to the front wheels, giving them a chance for traction. If the situation is critical, *one* hard application of the brakes will bring about the desired weight transfer. One word of caution: After deceleration, either with the throttle or the brake, be prepared for a skid. You may have induced too much weight transfer, causing the rear wheels to skid around. In this case, steer into the slide conventionally and keep your throttle feathered.

If you are carrying a heavy load in the rear seat or the trunk, your car may tend to oversteer at high speeds or on slippery pavement. If you experience this tail-end breakaway, steer into the skid and keep some power on. Your only hope is to keep the tail in line and steer through the bend. Slow down but do not get off the throttle entirely. This would eliminate all traction on the rear wheels and would send them looping to the outside of the curve.

We feel these emergency tactics are so crucial that the highlights of each should be repeated: Understeering cars (which includes most American and European passenger automobiles) will try to run straight off the road under emergency conditions. They need rapid deceleration to get them pointed in the right direction. Oversteering cars (the condition can be induced in an understeering car by excessive overloading) will lose traction at the rear wheels and will tend to spin. Steady power and corrective steering are necessary to overcome this situation.

On occasion a driver may enter a corner so fast that nothing will prevent him from shooting off the road. (Remember spinning the object around on the end of a string? The string just broke.) The driver is now faced with the unpleasant task of choosing a place to crash. This can reduce itself to selecting the lesser of two evils, such as ramming an oak tree or bounding across a plowed field. As we mentioned, try to exit from the highway as nearly in a straight line as possible and continue your efforts to bring the car under control. If at all possible, miss trees, because they are amazingly sturdy. If you have the instantaneous choice between a telephone pole and a tree of similar diameter, hit the pole. Dead wood is always weaker than live. When you get into such a situation, all thoughts of keeping the car unscathed should disappear. Life is at stake, and all actions should relate to their effect on you and your passengers, not on the automobile.

Many experts have blithely recommended that drivers relax as they are about to crash. This, they say, will make your body more resilient and less prone to broken bones. This is a wonderful idea, but telling a driver to relax in the face of a crash is about as sensible as asking a doomed man in the electric chair if he is comfortable. Don't count on being able to relax in an accident. Your mind and body will be operating at a fever pitch for these few seconds and you will find it very difficult to suddenly turn off your nerves and slouch back like a rag doll.

If you are driving, get a good grip on the steering wheel and hang on. Get set for a bucking, bounding ride that will make a Western bronco seem like a hobby horse. A seat belt will keep you in place, and it has been proved statistically that you have a much better chance of survival if you stay with the automobile, even if it should flip, than if you are thrown out.

As a passenger, it is best to brace your head and upper body against the dash. Do not make the mistake of grabbing a door handle. The consequences of a mistake like this are obvious.

Accidents occur with such stunning speed that you will probably experience a moment of confusion when the tumult subsides. Try to keep your composure until help arrives.

Before you get out of the automobile check to see if any power lines are down. If one is lying anywhere near the car, *stay put*. The next piece of metal you touch may send a deadly surge of electricity through your body.

Check first for injured people. If someone has been hurt, don't touch him if you can avoid it. Moving a person with a broken back or neck may be fatal, and in some instances you can be held liable. Cover the injured with a blanket or coat and call for help. Should someone be bleeding excessively, basic first-aid methods may help, but the most important thing to do is to notify the authorities. A highway emergency kit will be valuable on occasions like this. Outfitting one is inexpensive.

In the event the accident is minor, do your best to get the disabled cars clear of the highway so they will not pose a hazard to oncoming traffic.

Steering failure cannot be described as a common breakdown, but when it does occur, nothing can place the driver in a more hopeless position. There is only one thing to do: Stop. Normally a steering gear will not go entirely, and you will have some chance to get the automobile to the side of the road. If steering power should disappear altogether, all you can do is employ emergency braking procedures and pray.

Some people look upon a blowout as the beginning

of a certain wreck. Not so. Keep your wits and you will have no trouble surviving a blowout. *Stay off the brakes* at least until you get the automobile under control. The car will pull hard toward the side which has the crippled tire. Make steering corrections to keep the car going straight; the automobile will act cranky but it will obey if you persist and don't panic. Under ideal conditions coast to a stop at the roadside. If you have to stop rapidly, use the brakes *lightly,* because they will grab very easily.

The seriousness of brake failure depends on where it occurs. Should you lose your brakes on a steep hill, make no mistake about it, you are in trouble. Try to stop the car as quickly as possible rather than attempting to drive your way out of trouble. The longer you permit the car to roll, the more the momentum increases and the harder it will be to stop.

The first indication of brake failure is a limp pedal that goes to the floorboard. Try pumping the pedal vigorously to see if some stopping action can be activated. If you are not going too fast, drop into a lower range or gear. Be careful that speed is not excessive when you try the downshift. By dropping into a lower gear at high speeds you run the risk of blowing a clutch or even the engine through overrevving, and this will leave you without any engine braking. So if you're traveling over 60 mph, make a couple of applications of the parking brake to cut some of the velocity before trying a downshift.

The parking brake is linked independently with the rear wheels and will normally remain effective if the main system fails. However, use the parking brake sparingly because it is only half as powerful. If you just clamp it on in the event of brake failure, the stopping power will probably fade into nothing in a matter of seconds.

Don't hesitate to use roadside barriers for stopping, should your brakes fail. By swiping the side of the car along guardrails, fences, snowbanks, etc., you can reduce speed radically. Forget about ripping the side of the automobile off; without brakes your life is in jeopardy. Doors and fenders are cheap compared to your personal safety.

If you lose your brakes in heavy traffic, you should be able to downshift and come to a halt with the parking brake. Should this be impossible, hit the car ahead rather than risk a head-on collision by trying to pass. Because the relative speeds of your car and the one in front will be close, his bumper will cushion you to a stop without serious damage.

There is little or no excuse for having the brakes fail on modern automobiles. Such troubles can usually be traced to negligence on the part of the owner.

On reflection, it seems rather negative to devote all this space in a book about good driving to dangerous situations. But you would be only half prepared for the road if unpleasant subjects like this were not con-

sidered. And if you take a level-headed look at the
possible situations and are prepared to react coolly
under pressure, the odds that you get a "second
chance" from that "last chance" will increase immeas-
urably.

13

SOME WORDS OF CAUTION

It is not the aim of this book to strike fear into the reader. No one can be scared into being a good driver, and space devoted to gruesome details of shattering accidents is generally wasted. To be sure, automobile casualty rates are appalling, with about forty thousand deaths annually. But when it is remembered that the United States has almost as many drivers as the *combined* populations of England and France and that many of them have more horsepower under their right foot than that developed by most World War I airplanes, the overall quality of our driving becomes apparent.

Barring a national catastrophe, it is a certainty that we will soon have over one hundred million licensed drivers in the United States. Most of them will be sensible, responsible citizens behind the wheel, doing their best on highways that are likely to be badly overcrowded. But when we speak in astronomical figures like one hundred million, even *one* percent, or one million, irresponsible drivers can be a terrifying menace. Imagine if almost the entire populace of the state of Arizona suddenly took to the road and roamed the nation exhibiting every imaginable kind of dangerous and illegal driving tactic!

Despite the increase in drivers to more than one hundred million, there is a statistical probability that the death rate will not increase. Automobile casualties have diminished during the past quarter-century, while the number of drivers has doubled, and there is no reason to believe this trend will not continue.

Many tend to credit better automobiles and improved highways exclusively for keeping the traffic toll in check. Few people credit our drivers for having had any part in helping the situation. In fact, several years ago a slogan was circulated recommending that "you regard the other drivers on the road as madmen intent on killing you." How could anyone drive rationally with such a thought in mind?

The nation's drivers do a fine job in general, especially when one considers the demanding conditions under which many of them operate and the considerable bulk and power of the vehicles they handle. Granted, one in one hundred may be dangerous, but you cannot let that fact color your entire driving attitude. Never take the skill of other drivers for granted, but for goodness' sake don't cower from them. Most important, be sure *you* aren't that one person in one hundred who may cause the trouble!

It is one thing to be in an accident; it is another to know that you have caused it, especially if someone has been injured by your mistake. By observing the laws and using good judgment and restraint, you reduce the possibility of such a tragedy. In this connection we feel obligated to mention a few habits that must be avoided, habits that may be picked up by an otherwise good driver.

Never show off with your automobile. Resist this temptation! Anyone can squeal tires with almost any automobile. It takes very little power and very little skill to elicit a chirp from the rear wheels when you take off, so avoid this juvenile stunt. Aside from cutting tire mileage 10–15 miles *every* time you try it, it is an immediate indication of a poor driver. Remember—*anyone* can abuse an automobile.

The same applies to charging around street corners so quickly that the tires scream in protest. When you think about it, this is a pretty silly way to get attention. If you want people to notice you, wear a funny hat or grow a beard, but don't abuse your automobile and endanger others for the sake of a little attention.

Stay out of the stoplight Grand Prix circuit. Dragging at stoplights is probably the most useless sport in the world. It will gain you neither time nor satisfaction. If you believe you have a hot car, drive it to the nearest drag strip and take on some worthwhile competition under properly supervised conditions. In addition to being pointless, street dragging may cause a serious accident. Imagine yourself at a light, clutch in, engine revving, primed for the green to show so that you can leap ahead of the "field." The light changes and you scream into the intersection—smack into the path of somebody else trying to beat the light from the other direction.

Don't drive one-handed. Some people seem to think that the mark of a good driver is being as casual behind the wheel as possible. Maybe they are attempting to say, "Look how great I am with one hand. You ought to see me when I really try!" This of course is absurd. A good driver is always trying and that means both hands are on the wheel. The only place you will see an expert handling an automobile with one hand is in an auto thrill show. Here most maneuvers are executed one-handed for the sake of showmanship. And don't rely on knobs and spinners on the wheel to get you around tight corners. These devices will make you develop a distorted driving style, and they have been known to break in the middle of a corner, leaving the driver in a dangerous situation.

Don't try to punish other drivers for their mistakes. If another driver does something rude or inconsiderate, don't take it upon yourself to cut him off or crowd him onto the shoulder in retaliation. Your first reaction may be anger, and you will wish for the chance to give him a good dressing down for his incompetence. This being impossible in most instances, your next urge may be to blast your horn or ride inches off his rear bumper. Venting your frustration this way is both hazardous and futile. If another motorist cuts you off or forces you to take radical evasive action, don't try to discipline him. Leave that up to the police. If a thoughtless driver approaching you at night does not heed your warning blinks to lower his high beams, don't reciprocate by blinding him with yours. If you can't see where you're going, it's senseless to cut his vision out of spite. Risking a head-on collision is a poor way to prove a point.

There are certain things you would not do behind the wheel, things that plain common sense governs against. This should include drinking. *Do not, under any circumstances, mix driving with drinking.* If you are too young to drink, file this rule away for future reference. Should you be old enough, heed it if you value your financial independence and your personal freedom. For the average law-abiding individual, there is no quicker way to get into trouble than to disregard the above rule. Aside from heavy fines and possible loss of your license, civil lawsuits, arising from drunken driving accidents can put you in debt for the rest of your life. If you can't do anything else right on the road, at least listen to this warning. Every day the laws get tighter and the public's temper gets shorter with drunken drivers.

It doesn't take show-off tactics to abuse your automobile. There are several ways in which you can damage your car literally in your own backyard. For example, *don't drive your car hard until it has been thoroughly warmed up.* Depending on the weather, it may take the oil in your car's engine up to fifteen minutes to reach operating temperatures. Until then, the engine is not receiving proper lubrication and reciprocating parts are suffering. Under all conditions, give your engine a minimum of one or two minutes' warm-up after an overnight sit. If the weather is below freezing, the engine should have at least two or three minutes to warm up, *especially* if it is to be used in stop-start city driving. Then take it easy for the first few miles. This type of travel is much harder on an engine than steady open-road cruising, and a cool engine will be much more easily damaged. Be sure the warm-up is made at rpm's exceeding an idle because oil pressure is usually below normal at minimum engine speeds.

Make it a rule *never to let your engine idle* for more than a few seconds at a time. Whenever you are stopped (other than at a stoplight) with the engine running, actuate the throttle at short intervals to keep the revs above an idling speed. There is incomplete burning of fuel at an idle, and this causes the combustion chambers of the engine to become coated with coke and carbon. This has an adverse effect on spark plug life and the overall efficiency of the engine.

Keep the foregoing points in mind. If you are ever to develop the inner pride of being a really good driver, you must observe every "don't" we have mentioned.

Being able to climb from behind the wheel after a trip, no matter how short, and say to oneself, "I think I did my best," can provide genuine satisfaction. Try it.

14

A FEW AFTERTHOUGHTS

Selection of a car, be it new or used, should be based on more serious considerations than which model is the prettiest or which dealer will offer the best price. In the multitude of domestic and imported car types, there is one that will fit your needs, so try to make a choice on the basis of function, rather than form.

If you live in mountainous country with twisty roads and steep inclines, the car's brakes, transmission and suspension system should be major criteria. A person living in the plains states, with their sprawling expanses of flat, straight roadway, would be wise to think of automobiles which provide efficient operation at relatively high cruising speeds. Naturally the same sort of car might be out of place in the hands of a big-city commuter. Here a small compact or imported car would be the best bet for maneuverability and economy in the cramped urban traffic.

Should you be in the market for a new car, look beyond the glistening bodywork and the lush upholstery. Consider how adaptable each automobile is to your type of driving. Check the road tests in the motoring journals to learn what the automotive press thinks of the car in question. And, most important, drive it. If possible, spend at least two or three hours behind the wheel so that you can get really acquainted. No five-minute spin around the block will do this, so insist on your own test drive before buying.

Because each person has different requirements for an automobile, we will make no attempt to direct you toward this or that particular make. However, we would like to make this one recommendation: Before letting the dealer persuade you into the purchase of options that might be more ornamental than functional, be sure your new automobile is equipped with the most efficient brakes and the best suspension setup. Most manufacturers have special brake and suspension options available for slight extra charges. If you can purchase them on the model you have chosen, do so. The added stability and braking power will offset the few dollars added to the bill. Seat belts can be factory-installed for as little as $20, and at that price their omission is inexcusable.

Unfortunately not all of us are in a position to choose a new car, forcing us to check the used-car lots for our transportation. Here it takes a sharp eye to tell the good from the bad. A complete wreck may have been turned into a dazzling piece of machinery that will take your breath away with its good looks. The appearance of a used car should be one of the last considerations. A new coat of paint and $50 worth of bodywork can turn 75 percent of the cars on the road today into absolute jewels, so watch out.

Look over every part of the running gear. (If you don't feel qualified, have a mechanic do the job; it will be worth the expense.) Check the tires for uneven wear that may indicate poor wheel alignment. Test the shock absorbers and look for play in the steering wheel. Let the engine idle and watch the exhaust pipe. If you spot blue smoke, look elsewhere, because the engine is burning oil. Poor wiring can cause unending headaches, so take a look under the instrument panel. If it looks as if a flock of sparrows live there, don't buy.

Get underneath the body and look for places where welding has been done. This may mean the automobile has been in a serious crash, so be extra cautious. If you live in northern climates, investigate the lower body panels for heavy rust that may be covered by a thin coat of paint.

Pull the oil dipstick out and check the condition of the lubricant. Should the oil seem like a particularly heavy grade, beware, because it may have been put in the engine to muffle noisy bearings. Be sure to check for defective bearings on the road. Normally they will reveal themselves with a harsh metallic hammering from the innards of the engine. A bad connecting-rod bearing will usually make noise when the car is decelerated. Main bearings will hammer when the engine is under a load, as when climbing an incline or accelerating (in certain situations rod bearings may make noise under load too). If you hear any suspicious noises in these situations, forget about the car. Defective bearings mean terrific repair bills under any circumstances.

Should you be trying a standard transmission automobile, put on the parking brake while stopped and engage third gear, then engage the clutch slowly. If the engine slows down and finally stalls, the clutch is holding adequately. But if the clutch can be engaged without snuffing out the engine, the unit is slipping badly. Watch for any loud clunking sounds when operating an automatic transmission automobile because these usually mean high-cost problems.

Turning back the odometer is a favorite trick of many used-car dealers, even reputable ones. Check the floormats, the driver's seat and the pedals for an indication of mileage. If an automobile has only 18,000 miles on the clock, yet the seat sags and the pedals and floormat are badly scuffed, something is fishy. Should all the numbers on the odometer appear out of line, it is likely the mileage has been tampered with.

When buying a used car, try to pick an established dealer and stay away from junk cars. Older machines will only cost you money. Shy away from the more exotic used cars, unless they are practically brand new. You may be asking for trouble if you purchase a five- or six-year-old car equipped with such goodies as power brakes, steering, windows, etc. Most power equipment is very reliable, but on an ancient automobile such devices only add to the maintenance costs. If possible, stick to "basic transportation" when shopping for used cars.

Stay away from the flashy 300-hp models when buying your first automobile. Too much horsepower in the hands of an inexperienced driver can only mean trouble. Start out with a small, simple machine, preferably with a manual transmission. Top pilots didn't begin to fly in jet fighters but in slower training planes, where they learned the basics of flight. If you have aspirations of being a top-notch driver, start your career in a "trainer" too.

Every year more young Americans are becoming the owners of automobiles. In many high schools across the nation, the students' parking lot is filled with much more impressive machinery than that driven by the faculty. We have no objection to a young boy or girl having his or her own car, provided it is driven responsibly. However, automobiles should be treated as luxuries by young people and should not be handed out by parents as part of their normal allowance.

Young people in high school should *earn* their cars. This can be done in a variety of ways and need not be on a dollar-and-cents basis. The most important thing is that a car should be the reward for solid hard work on the part of its young owner.

A number of nationwide studies have been made concerning the relationship of poor scholarship in high school with the ownership of automobiles. The results provide strong evidence that real self-control is needed on the part of the teen-age driver to keep his marks from slipping. If you are still in high school and operate a car, spend at least two hours studying for every sixty minutes with the automobile. You should be mature enough to accept this sort of responsibility. If not, you are too young to handle a car on today's highways.

Probably the best possible way for a young person, especially a boy, to get a car is to build it. The fellow who takes an automobile and reconstructs it from the ground up is putting his heart and soul into that machine. Every part will have been selected with care and installed with pride.

As a driver, you are part of a long heritage of the American road. That heritage includes such exciting names as Ford, Chrysler, Marmon, Cord, Kettering, Olds, DePalma, Vanderbilt, Firestone, and many others who have left their mark on the very automobile you drive. Without their labors, you might still be traveling on horseback. It was their dream that the automobile should mean more than merely a drab utility like a washing machine or a vacuum cleaner. An automobile in the right hands is a vibrant thing that responds and moves like a thoroughbred horse. But it needs something more than just someone to steer it. It needs a driver who will communicate with it, a driver who is able to establish a link between mind and machine.

Watch how enthusiasts treat their automobiles. They handle them with the respect that is due a fine piece of machinery. If you are able to take pride in your automobile, you will take more pride in yourself and in your driving. A man at peace with himself has nothing to prove on the highway except that he is in command of his wits and his automobile.

As with everything else, you will get no more out of your automobile and your driving than you are willing to put into them. Treat your car like a beast of burden and it will treat you like a wagonmaster; abuse it and it will lash back at you like a wild animal; despise it and it will despise you; fear it and it will overwhelm you. Give all that you can to driving and your automobile will work with you, as a good horse and jockey work together. When you begin to sense this union between yourself and your car, driving will become the wonderfully pleasurable and meaningful experience that it was meant to be.

May your miles on the road be safe and happy miles.

INDEX

179